SURVIVAL OR PROPHECY?

SURVIVAL OR PROPHECY?

THE LETTERS OF THOMAS MERTON

AND JEAN LECLERCQ

EDITED BY BROTHER PATRICK HART

FOREWORD BY ARCHBISHOP REMBERT G. WEAKLAND

FARRAR, STRAUS AND GIROUX

NEW YORK

Farrar, Straus and Giroux
19 Union Square West, New York 10003

Compilation, editorial work, and introduction copyright
© 2002 by Farrar, Straus and Giroux, LLC
Letters of Jean Leclercq copyright © 2002 by the
Abbaye St-Maurice, Luxembourg
Foreword copyright © 2002 by Rembert G. Weakland
All rights reserved
Distributed in Canada by Douglas & McIntyre Ltd.
Printed in the United States of America
First edition, 2002

Library of Congress Cataloging-in-Publication Data
Merton, Thomas, 1915–1968.
    Survival or prophecy? : the letters of Thomas Merton and Jean
Leclercq ; edited by Brother Patrick Hart ; foreword by
Archbishop Rembert G. Weakland.
        p.   cm.
    Includes bibliographical references and index.
    ISBN 0-374-27206-9 (hc : alk. paper)
    1. Merton, Thomas, 1915–1968—Correspondence.   2. Trappists—
United States—Correspondence.   3. Leclercq, Jean, 1911–
—Correspondence.   4. Benedictines—Luxembourg—Correspondence.
I. Leclercq, Jean, 1911–   .   II. Hart, Patrick.   III. Title.

BX4705.M542 A4 2002
271'.1022—dc21

                                                    2002019785

Designed by Jonathan D. Lippincott

www.fsgbooks.com

1   3   5   7   9   10   8   6   4   2

Frontispiece: Jean Leclercq and Thomas Merton in Bangkok,
December 1968

The vocation of the monk in the modern world . . . is not survival but prophecy.

    —Thomas Merton to Jean Leclercq, July 23, 1968

CONTENTS

✠

FOREWORD

Searching out the reasons for the flowering of monasticism after World War II, whether in the United States or in other parts of the New World, involves studying the voluminous writings of its proponents in that period. Among them, Thomas Merton and Jean Leclercq take pride of place. Merton, the Cistercian, stayed close to his cloister in Kentucky; Leclercq, the Benedictine, traveled the world over. But both were in touch with monastic happenings everywhere in the world and influenced both the thinking and the aspirations of the monks of their day. To the general public in the United States Merton is the better known. However, one can see from this correspondence his deferential bearing toward Leclercq, who was his senior by only four years and who was better known among scholars and monasteries of Africa, Asia, and Europe.

Jean Leclercq went to everybody and every place on the globe; everyone came to Thomas Merton at Gethsemani. Yet from the letters it is clear that the two men were following similar paths and had similar aspirations for the future of monasticism.

Elected Abbot Primate of the Benedictine Order in 1967, a role that required much travel and attendance at many conferences on the future of monasticism, I came to know Leclercq well through the years. The first opportunity I had to come to know Merton personally was in Bangkok in 1968, a meeting that brought Merton and Leclercq together and was the occasion of Merton's unexpected and sudden death. Of the two, Leclercq was easier to know and converse with. He was a delightful extrovert, not too complicated psychologically, and conversant on everything and everybody. His English was good, even if clipped in the French style. He could be blunt, but never rude. Like the monks of the Middle Ages, whom he studied so assiduously, he seemed to regard his learning as but the support system for his interest in contemporary monastic renewal. He had no "authority complex," and for me, even though I was the titular head of his Order, being with him was always a delight.

Merton was harder to come to know. He was psychologically quite complicated, full of inner quarrels about his public role and his monastic calling, and although he wrote a great deal about his interior spiritual life and about his opinions on many matters, he was much more reserved in speaking—at least around me, an authority figure.

What the two men had in common was their flair for writing. They poured out books and articles over several decades. They both wrote many letters—Leclercq's output reaching about sixteen hundred items! Merton wrote personal diaries or journals; Leclercq did not. Yet Leclercq's notes, written during his many visits to Africa and Asia but not meant for publication, were similar to journals, if perhaps less personal and more "objective." Reading Leclercq's letters is like being in a privileged observatory that affords a view of everyone and every place in the monastic world of his day.

What characterized this new flowering of monasticism in the postwar period, and what gave it such a vibrant new impetus?

The postwar monastic renewal was vitalized, first of all, by the "return to the sources." This renewal was not a complete rejection of the previous monastic renewal, that of the nineteenth century, but it did not rely explicitly on the "masters" of that first renewal. Dom Columba Marmion's *Christ the Ideal of the Monk* (English ed., 1922) and Dom Paul Delatte's *The Rule of Saint Benedict: A Commentary* (English ed., 1921) were not forgotten, but, as we see in reading the letters between Merton and Leclercq, these works were not considered a common source for renewal, even though they were well known in all monasteries of the French tradition. The German monastic writers of the nineteenth and early twentieth centuries—for example, Ildefons Herwegen (d. 1946), Odo Casel (d. 1948), and Anselm Stolz (d. 1942)—were likewise known but more or less ignored, as were the remarkable historical studies of David Knowles in England.

Rather, the driving force behind the postwar renewal was a return to older sources, to the origins of monasticism in the patristic period and to St. Bernard and the Cistercian reforms of the twelfth century. Merton and Leclercq had a common interest in these sources and saw them as pivotal for monastic reform in their day. Thus they so easily and eagerly shared in their correspondence new facets of the life and personality of Bernard and new insights into the early Cistercian ideals of community, solitude, the Rule, and the like. They approached history in the same way: as a vital source for the renewal of monastic life in their times. They hoped that a return to these monastic ideals of Bernard's day would be replicable in their own and felt it was absolutely necessary for any revival of monasticism.

Merton and Leclercq were not alone in thinking so. To make the picture of this monastic renewal in the second half of the twentieth century complete, one would have to add to the list of significant monastic authors the remarkable scholar Adalbert de Vogüé, O.S.B. His voluminous writings on the Rule of Benedict and its historical precedents were yet another source for this new flowering. A monk of La Pierre-qui-Vire, de Vogüé taught for many years in the Monastic Institute at Sant'Anselmo in Rome and thus, with Leclercq, influenced several generations of monks in the second half of the twentieth century.

Merton and Leclercq were well versed in the Latin Fathers but admitted their deficiencies in knowledge of Greek monastic writers. This lacuna in postwar monastic renewal was filled in by the magisterial writings of Jean Gribomont, O.S.B., a confrère of Dom Leclercq and also a professor at Sant'Anselmo at that time. The many students who were taught by Leclercq and these other masters brought back to their monasteries everywhere in the world the notion of a return to the original sources—a *ressourcement*—which has guided monastic reform ever since. Merton and Leclercq were a part of this larger movement and had the advantage of strong convictions on how the ideals of those earlier periods were to be carried out in our day.

The other vital influence on the post–World War II monastic renewal was Asian monasticism. Leclercq had a great curiosity and a superficial and practical acquaintance with the Asian monastic traditions (Buddhist, Hindu, and the like); Merton had a more accurate theoretical knowledge but lacked contact with the living Asian monastic tradition. That is why his trip to Asia in 1968 was so important to him. His encounters with Tibetan monks in Dharamsala, with Buddhist monks of the Theravada tradition in India, and then with Asian Catholic monks in Bangkok were the fruit of a dialogue he had carried on inwardly and through his writings for more than a decade. Thus stimulated, the dialogue has continued in both East and West and, in its own way, has prompted Western monks to study their tradition's more contemplative sources in a desire to compare them with Asian manifestations. In this regard, the most important person responsible for bringing the two together was not Merton—he did not live long enough to do so—but Dom Bede Griffiths (d. 1993), who lived the mixture of the two veins of monasticism, East and West, in his own ashram and who was, in turn, to influence many other Western monks. He had an authenticity about him that came from lived experience that neither Leclercq nor Merton could match.

In reading the letters between Leclercq and Merton, one is struck by the influence that the young monasteries in Africa were having on the monastic renewal in the West. The descriptions given by Leclercq I can personally verify. During the many trips I made to Africa and the nascent monasteries there, I felt that I was returning to the early days of monasticism. There the Rule of Benedict could be lived out without perceptible adaptations and without commentary and added "by-laws." This return to simplicity continues to influence monastic renewal into the twenty-first century.

Both Merton and Leclercq accepted without question the best in modern biblical exegesis, using it to complement their patristic and medieval approaches. For monks, the new biblical scholarship was an important postwar phenomenon, a scriptural aid to the "return to the sources." The rediscovery of the Benedictine *lectio divina*—a spirituality grounded in prayer that rose out of sustained attention to the scriptural texts—was not marked by a rejection of modern biblical insights that came from the new historical and form criticism, that is, from a new knowledge of the ways the Scriptures had been redacted from various fragmentary and often contradictory sources. Instead, these insights were integrated into the whole, producing a more biblically informed spirituality.

One could say the same about their approach to modern psychological advances. Merton in particular, perhaps because of his role as novice master at Gethsemani, which left him in charge of new monks' character formation, became quite fluent in these insights and applied them everywhere in his spirituality and in his writings. Neither author is antiscience or antimodern per se. Perhaps this is one reason why both were so appealing to the younger generation in the 1960s and 1970s. Their criticisms of modern culture had more to do with its lack of deeper and life-giving values than with its scientific advances, which they recognized and welcomed.

Both Merton and Leclercq saw an advantage in renewing in the Church the vocation of the hermit, so characteristic of Catholic monasticism in the early days of the Church, but discouraged later on. The reemergence of hermits seemed a strange phenomenon to many in those postwar years. Merton in particular felt misunderstood whenever he mentioned his desire to live as a hermit among the Camaldolese in Europe or in a simple dwelling in the woods near the Abbey of Gethsemani. Reading about Merton's struggle within his own monastery to realize this vocation for himself can be a bit tedious, but it is a significant part of the monastic renewal and its more patristic roots. Although Leclercq did not have the disposition or desire for the eremitical life, he appreciated it very much, influenced by his remarkable Abbot at Clervaux, Dom Jacques Winandy. Leclercq defended this vocation in higher places and changed the attitude of many Superiors toward it. Their work was not without fruit. The possibility of the eremitical life was favorably treated in the revised Code of Canon Law (1983), and Catholic hermits are now found all over the world.

Finally, both authors, but especially Merton, saw their roles as prophetic witnesses. Perhaps the most attractive aspect of Merton's concept of monastic renewal was his interpretation of the *fuga mundi* (the flight from the world) not as a selfish and individualistic withdrawal from the trials and troubles of the world around him but as a "monastic distancing" of himself to help to bring about positive change in contemporary society. His criticisms of the United States and the culture of his day are acerbic and in the spirit of the prophets of old. He felt free, through his monastic vocation and the detachment from worldly life it offered, to make such judgments. Leclercq was less prone to negative assertions, but he was not without his sharp and unbending criticisms of European culture and European monasticism in particular.

The prophetic stance was one of the enduring and most attractive aspects of the monastic renewal in the last half of the twentieth century; and both Merton and Leclercq, cognizant that the Christian monastic tradition had first emerged as a form of prophetic witness against the ever more worldly Church, brought it to bear on the Church of their own day. They knew that the early monks had felt a need to witness to the Church first of all, especially against its tendency to compromise with the demands of the Empire and against its desire to seek power and prestige; and they sought to make such a witness with their own lives. The passion of many youthful candidates to monastic life, as well as many laypeople seeking deeper spiritual values in ordinary life, suggests the great appeal of this sort of witness, especially when described by a writer of Merton's caliber.

The publication of the letters of Jean Leclercq in the summer of 2000 and the final volumes of the complete journals of Thomas Merton in 1998 is proof enough that there is still a lively interest in the works of these two remarkable monks—their thoughts, their aspirations, their deep love of the monastic ideal, and their blueprint for its renewal in our times. It is only fitting that the correspondence between them also sees the light of day. It is clear that their influence has lasted into this new century and will perdure.

Archbishop Rembert G. Weakland

INTRODUCTION

☩

When the history of twentieth-century monasticism comes to be written, it is hard not to think that two monks will dominate the story: Thomas Merton and Jean Leclercq.   —Bernard McGinn*

The correspondence between Dom Jean Leclercq and Father Thomas Merton is a microcosmic history of the monastic renewal in the mid-twentieth century. When the exchange began between these two monks separated by the Atlantic Ocean, Thomas Merton was a Cistercian monk recently ordained to the priesthood (1949), already well known as a result of the phenomenal success of *The Seven Storey Mountain*, and becoming more and more involved with the monastic formation of the young monks at the Abbey of Gethsemani in Kentucky. Meanwhile, Jean Leclercq, in the

*From *The Joy of Learning and the Love of God: Essays in Honor of Jean Leclercq*, edited by E. Rozanne Elder (Kalamazoo, Mich.: Cistercian Publications, 1995).

Benedictine monastery of Clervaux in Luxembourg, was publishing articles on medieval monastic writers, preparing for the day when he would begin his work on the critical edition of the works of St. Bernard of Clairvaux. So, naturally, the first letters dealt mainly with traditional monastic questions, but this later broadened to include renewal, social justice, experimental monasticism in Third World countries, ecumenism, and the place of the monk in an increasingly troubled world.

The first exchanges concerned making a microfilm of some texts of St. Bernard that were discovered among the manuscripts of the Obrecht Collection at the Abbey of Gethsemani. Some seventy manuscripts and the same number of incunabula were eventually transferred from the Gethsemani vault to the Institute of Cistercian Studies Library at Western Michigan University in Kalamazoo. From the earliest letters it becomes evident that some letters are missing. In any case, Merton uses the occasion to invite Leclercq to come to Gethsemani the next time he is in the States.

In a Foreword to Bruno Scott James's volume of selected letters of St. Bernard of Clairvaux, Thomas Merton wrote what could be an autobiographical statement regarding his monastic exchange of letters with Jean Leclercq: "The whole Bernard is not to be found in his letters alone: but the whole Bernard can never be known without them." Merton concluded his Foreword with these equally revealing words: "Let us at least gather from St. Bernard that letter-writing is an art which has been forgotten, but which needs to be re-learned."* St. Bernard carried on a vast correspon-dence in the twelfth century, even to the reigning Pope Eugenius III, a Cistercian monk whom Bernard consid-ered his spiritual son. His reputation as a mediator be-tween church and state has never been rivaled. He was truly "the last of the Fathers." For both Leclercq and Merton, St. Bernard was the preeminent embodiment of the Cistercian tradition with its human depth and contemplative wisdom.

What I find especially significant in regard to Merton's side of the correspondence is how he kept ma-turing both as a person and as a monk. It was un-doubtedly due to his contact with persons like Jean Leclercq that his thinking evolved regarding monastic renewal and the essential place of the monk in the mod-ern world. Robert Giroux, Merton's friend from his Co-lumbia days and later his editor, spoke of this aspect of Merton's development at the dedication of the new Thomas Merton Center at Bellarmine University, in Louisville, Kentucky, on October 10, 1997: "I have known many gifted writers, but none who developed and grew as fast and as deeply as Merton did."[†]

Dom Jean Leclercq was born in Avesnes, in northern France on January 31, 1911 (the same day as Merton, but four years earlier); Thomas Merton was born in Prades, in southern France, at the foothills of the Pyre-

*From Thomas Merton's Foreword to *St. Bernard of Clairvaux*, by Bruno Scott James (Chicago: Henry Regnery Company, 1953), pp. v–viii.
[†]*The Merton Seasonal: A Quarterly Review* 23, no. 1 (Spring 1998).

nees, in 1915. Leclercq entered the monastery of Clervaux in 1928. After monastic studies and ordination to the priesthood, he became one of the most prolific historians of medieval Benedictines and Cistercians. (See the Appendix for a chronology of the main events of his life as well as the principal books he published on medieval subjects.) He was one of the best-loved scholars throughout his long career, which ended at his Abbey of Clervaux on October 27, 1993.

Although Leclercq was not eremitically inclined, he was open to the hermit life as an exception to the general rule in cenobitic monasteries; from his historical research he knew it was not foreign to the tradition. He encouraged Merton and others who he felt had a special vocation to a more solitary way of life, but within the framework of traditional monasticism, both Benedictine and Cistercian. Leclercq's responses to Merton's desire for greater solitude were always tempered with prudence and caution, and in obedience to the local Abbot. On the Feast of St. Bernard, August 20, 1965, Father Louis (as Merton was known among the monks) was finally granted permission to enter the hermit life full-time in a small hermitage on the property of the Abbey of Gethsemani. When in America, Leclercq frequently visited Gethsemani to give talks to the community and to evaluate Merton's solitary vocation at close range.

In early 1968, after Dom James Fox resigned his abbatial office at Gethsemani and Father Flavian Burns was elected his successor, Leclercq continued his contacts, and was instrumental in arranging for the invitation for Merton to participate in the conference of Asian monastic Superiors in Bangkok, Thailand, in December 1968. Leclercq and Merton met there for the last time. It was especially fitting that this final meeting of monastic friends took place in the midst of Asian monks and nuns gathered to discuss ideas the two of them cherished—the need to explore monasticism in the Far East and to take advantage of the wisdom of non-Christian monastic traditions of Asia for the sake of a revitalized monasticism in the West.

In the last letter that Merton addressed to Leclercq in this exchange, dated July 23, 1968, he writes: "The vocation of the monk in the modern world, especially Marxist, is not survival but prophecy. We are all too busy saving our skins."

Thomas Merton was electrocuted by a faulty standing fan in his Bangkok room only a few hours after he delivered his talk on monasticism and Marxism to the assembled monks and nuns on December 10, 1968. Rembert G. Weakland, who was then Abbot Primate of the Benedictines, presided at the conference and gave the homily at the funeral liturgy in Bangkok, in which he eulogized Merton as a true monk at heart, always restless in his never-ending search for God, always moving forward to that farther shore. The same could be said of Jean Leclercq, who through his intellectual explorations never gave up the search for the one thing necessary.

It is our hope that this unique monastic exchange of

letters will help readers to understand the essential meaning of this radical response to the Gospel, incarnated so well by these two gifted monks, and how we can in our turn live the call of Christian discipleship more authentically in the years to come.

Brother Patrick Hart

EDITOR'S NOTE

Several of the early letters of Jean Leclercq were written in French. In the years before his death Dom Leclercq entrusted the translations to his English-speaking secretary, Sister Bernard Said, O.S.B. After Leclercq's death several more letters written in French were discovered; Father Chrysogonus Waddell, O.C.S.O., of Gethsemani Abbey was asked to translate these into English. Our thanks to both Sister Bernard and Father Chrysogonus for providing the translations.

In transcribing the letters, we have followed the editorial policy established in previous volumes of Thomas Merton's letters of inserting translations of foreign expressions in brackets. We have used headnotes and footnotes only when it was deemed essential to explain the context or a missing letter.

Thanks to numerous persons who have assisted us in this venture, especially Dom Michel Jorrot, the Benedictine Abbot of Jean Leclercq's monastery of Saint-Maurice in Clervaux, Luxembourg, for forwarding to me the entire correspondence that was found among Leclercq's papers following his death in 1993. A word of gratitude to Brothers Stephen Batchelor, Anton Rusnak, and Columban Weber of Gethsemani, who made up for my incompetence in the realm of computer skills. Finally, I am deeply indebted to Robert Giroux and Paul Elie of Farrar, Straus and Giroux, who were a great source of encouragement as the work progressed to a happy conclusion.

LETTERS

This first extant letter from Dom Jean Leclercq to Father Louis (Thomas Merton) opens with a reference to a letter from Merton dated January 15, 1950. Apparently, the lost letter to Leclercq from Merton was in regard to what current research was being done on the Cistercian Fathers. Dom Leclercq was interested in the Gethsemani manuscripts that were kept in a vault until they were transferred to the Institute of Cistercian Studies Library at Western Michigan University in Kalamazoo a decade later.

Munich

January 28, 1950

I am happy that you are doing a study on a collection of texts by St. Bernard. Never enough can be done to make him known, and it answers a real need of our contemporaries: a Swiss editor has also just asked me for a collection in German.

I am also in contact with the Reverend Bruno Scott James.

I will be happy to look over your *Collectanea* [*Cisterciensia*] articles when I get a copy of the issue. I think that the only important book about St. Bernard these last years was the one by [William] Watkins, *St. Bernard of Clairvaux*, which I mention in the bibliographical note in *S. Bernard mystique*. There is also a fine chapter in *Aufgang des Abendlandes* by Heer, ed. Europa, Wien [Vienna] and Zurich.

I studied Baldwin of Ford some time ago, especially his doctrine on the Eucharist, for a collection which did not appear, but I do not think that anyone has done any work on Baldwin since then.

So there is still a great deal to do, and I think that the Lord is expecting a great deal from a true monastic life in our own days and that the world stands in need of it. So you have a beautiful mission. I would be happy to receive your books; I have heard them spoken about. If I can help you in anything, I am at your service, and I ask you to believe, my Reverend Father, in my devoted respect in Our Lord.

JEAN LECLERCQ TO THOMAS MERTON

Lisbon

[Undated—before Easter, 1950]

I did receive the films of your manuscripts of St. Bernard, and I thank you. The film of the *Sermones in Cantica* [Sermons on the Song of Songs] will be used very soon. Unfortunately, the film of the *Sermones* is unreadable; the photo is blurred.

I have not yet returned to Clervaux, where your books are waiting for me. I know that they arrived there, but I have not yet had a chance to read them. I have only seen your articles in *Collectanea Cisterciensia* on the mystical doctrine of St. Bernard. I will read them when I can do so. I am sure, according to what I have heard, that you have gone much deeper than I have into the mystical life and doctrine of St. Bernard. This I have done only very superficially. But perhaps later on, when I have finished the edition, I will be able to do something more mature, after having spent a long time with the texts.

For the moment I am leading a life completely contrary to my vocation and to my ideal, and the cause of it is St. Bernard. I am traveling all over Europe looking for manuscripts. They are everywhere. But this documentation has to be assembled once for all, and it can be hoped that St. Bernard will come out of it better known. It is an extremely difficult job. It is a major scientific responsibility, especially at certain times. For example, soon I am going to have to decide which manuscripts are to be retained to establish the text of the *Sermones in Cantica*: all the work that follows will depend on this decision. Please pray that this work be done well and that it be worthy of St. Bernard.

THOMAS MERTON TO JEAN LECLERCQ

A decade before Vatican II, Thomas Merton was already returning to the sources of monasticism with his conferences on Benedict, Cassian, Pachomius,

Evagrius, and other writers of the earliest tradition. He was also moving into the twelfth-century Cistercian "evangelists": Bernard of Clairvaux, William of Saint-Thierry, Guerric of Igny, and Aelred of Rievaulx.

April 22, 1950

Another film of the St. Bernard Sermons is now on the way to you. This time I looked it over to see if it was all right and it was legible on our machine. I am sorry the first attempt was not too good: you must forgive our young students who are just trying their hand at this kind of work for the first time. Pray that they may learn, because in the future many demands will be made on their talents—if any.

I might wish that your travels would bring you to this side of the Atlantic and that we might have the pleasure of receiving you at Gethsemani. We have just remodeled the vault where our rare books are kept and have extended its capacities to include a good little library on Scripture and the Fathers and the Liturgy—or at least the nucleus of one. Here I hope to form a group of competent students not merely of history or of the texts but rather—in line with the tradition which you so admirably represent—men competent in all-round spiritual theology, as well as scholarship, using their time and talents to develop the seed of the Word of God in their souls, not to choke it under an overgrowth of useless research as is the tradition in the universities of this country at the moment. I fervently hope that somehow we shall see in America men who are able to produce something like *Dieu Vivant* [a French journal]. Cistercians will never be able to do quite that, I suppose, but we can at least give a good example along those lines. Our studies and writing should by their very nature contribute to our contemplation, at least remotely, and contemplation in turn should be able to find expression in channels laid open for it and deepened by familiarity with the Fathers of the Church. This is an age that calls for St. Augustines and Leos, Gregorys and Cyrils!

That is why I feel that your works are so tremendously helpful, dear Father. Your *St. Bernard mystique* is altogether admirable because, while being simple and fluent, it communicates to the reader a real appreciation of St. Bernard's spirituality. You are wrong to consider your treatment of St. Bernard superficial. It is indeed addressed to the general reader, but for all that it is profound and all-embracing and far more valuable than the rather technical study which I undertook for *Collectanea* [*Cisterciensia*] and which, as you will see on reading it, was beyond my capacities as a theologian. The earlier sections especially, in my study, contain many glaring and silly errors—or at least things are often very badly expressed there.* If I write a book on the saint I shall try to redeem myself, without entering into the technical discussions that occupy M. Gilson in his rather brilliant study.† But there again, a book of your type is far more helpful.

---

*Thomas Merton, "The Transforming Union in St. Bernard and St. John of the Cross," *Collectanea Cisterciensia* 10 (1948), pp. 107, 210; 11 (1949), pp. 41, 351; 12 (1950), p. 25.
†Etienne Gilson, *The Mystical Theology of Saint Bernard* (New York: Sheed & Ward, 1940).

Be sure that we are praying for the work you now have in hand, which is so important and which implies such a great responsibility for you.

I had heard that you were helping to prepare for the press Dom Wilmart's edition of Ailred's *De institutione inclusarum* [Institution for recluses] but perhaps you have put this on the shelf for the time being. Are the Cistercians of the Common Observance editing the works of Ailred? Where are they doing so and when is the work expected to be finished? By the way, about the spelling of Ailred: the most prominent English scholars seem to be spelling him as I have just done, with an "i." I wish there could be some unity on this point. My work on him is in abeyance at the moment, but when I get on with it I suppose I had better go on using this spelling. What do you think about that?

Rest assured, dear Father, that I am praying for you and that our students are doing the same. Please pray for us too. I have too much activity on my shoulders, teaching and writing.

JEAN LECLERCQ TO THOMAS MERTON

Both Leclercq and Merton stressed the essential contemplative nature of monasticism and were interested in getting back to the original charism of the founders of monasticism, which made the contemplative life the monastic ideal. The Cistercian tradition, beginning with the foundation of Cîteaux in 1098, had its roots in previous Benedictine reforms, such as those of St. Benedict of Aniane, and actually could be traced back to the earlier tradition with Athanasius, Cassian, and Pachomius.

Clervaux

May 5, 1950

I was just going to write to you when I received, yesterday, your last letter. Thank you for the new film, which has already arrived.

Thank you also for your prayers and encouragement. I know that some scholars and professors criticize my books because they are too "human," not sufficiently, not purely "scientific," objective: but I do not care about having a good reputation as a scholar among scholars, although I could also do pure scholarly work, and I sometimes do, just to show that I know what it is. But I also know that many monks, and they are the more monastic monks, in several Orders—Camaldolese, Cistercians, Trappists, Benedictines of the strictest observances—find my books nourishing, and find in them an answer to their own aspirations. I thank God for that. My only merit—if any—is to accept not to be a pure scholar; otherwise I never invent ideas: I just bring to light ideas and experiences which are to be found in old monastic books that nobody, even in monasteries, ever reads today.

Since you seem to want me to do so, I am sending you today some offprints, just about "monastica." As you will see, I always say and write the same thing, because only one is necessary, and it is the only thing you would find in old monastic texts . . .

I think you have an important job to do at Gethsemani, first for America, and then for the whole Cistercian Order: to come back to the Cistercian idea. But there are two difficulties. The first is to keep the just measure in work, either manual or intellectual. Both forms of work, especially the second, entail a danger of activism (mental activism): that is a personal question which each monk has to solve for himself if he wants to work and stay a monk; some are unable to do both and have to choose to remain monks. The second difficulty is more of the historical order, if we want to study the Cistercian tradition. I am alluding to the illusion of believing that the Cistercian tradition began with Cîteaux. I am becoming more and more convinced that the Cistercian tradition cannot be understood without its roots in pre-existing and contemporary Benedictine—and generally monastic—tradition. That is why in my studies I never separate the different forms and expressions of the unique monastic thought and experience. For instance, if one begins to study the Mariology of the Cistercian school without taking into consideration previous and contemporary monastic thought at the same time about the Virgin, then one tends to think that the Cistercians were at the origin of all true and fervent Mariology. Yet if one recalls what St. Anselm and the monks of the Anglo-Norman eleventh century wrote, then possibly one might come to the conclusion that in this field Cistercians, far from making progress, may even have retrograded (I think, for example, of the Conception of Our Lady). The only way to avoid such pitfalls is to be quite free from any order-emphasis, any "order-politics," and to search solely for the truth in the life of the Church of God.

Since you ask me what I think about your books, then I tell you, even though I am no special authority on the matter. I suppose that the condition of our relations resides in perfect sincerity and loyalty.

I arrived back at Clervaux a few days ago, and have just had time to read the Prologue and the first two chapters of *The Waters of Siloe*. I shall read the rest and then tell you my impressions. So far, I must say that I thoroughly enjoy your pages: both what you say and the way you say it. I think that one immediately feels that you "believe" in the contemplative life, and this faith of yours is more forceful for convincing your readers than would be the most scientific treatment of the subject.

In my opinion, you point out the very essence of monastic life when you say that it is a contemplative life. The Benedictine tradition is certainly a contemplative tradition: the doctrine of Benedictine medieval writers (and almost always up to our own days—the twentieth century is an exception, alas!) is a doctrine of contemplation and contemplative life. But we must confess that Benedictine history is not entirely—and in certain periods not at all—contemplative. Nevertheless, even when Benedictines were busy about many things, they never made this business *circa plurima* [about many things] an ideal, and they never spoke about it; their doctrine was always that of the *unum necessarium* [the one thing necessary].

I think you are quite right when you say that we fall short of this ideal for want of simplicity. There have always been—and there still are today—attempts to get back to this simplicity. And one such attempt has always been writing. But the danger is always there, and even today Cistercians do not always succeed in avoiding it. For instance, from the Cistercian—and even simple monastic—point of view, Orval (the new Orval)* has been and remains a scandal. It is a sin against simplicity: first because it is luxurious, and then because, on pretext of observing the Statutes forbidding gold and certain other materials, they have used precious and exotic materials which give the same impression as would gold, without being gold, and so on. And the festival held in honor of the consecration of Orval was also scandalous and has been felt as such even by Cistercians and Trappists. In the same way, the noise and publicity made over Gethsemani on the occasion of its centenary, and the write-up in magazines that had, in the same issue, pictures of pin-up girls, were also scandalous and have been felt as such (but perhaps that was in keeping with the "American style"). You see, dear Reverend Father, that I do not spare you. But it is in order to show how great is the temptation.

I find your pages about Rome perfectly sincere and

---

*A royal monastery in southern Belgium. Since the king and queen were buried there, the place took on something of the character of a tourist attraction.

just. I am glad that you were allowed to write so freely. Others, I know, have not had that same liberty, nor do they even now. But I hope that the love of truth will make people surrender all "order-orthodoxy" and "order-politics."

I know the Procurator General of the S.O.C. [Sacred Order of Cistercians, or Cistercians of the Common Observance], Abbot [Matthaeus] Quatember, very well. He has, in my opinion, a good idea of what Cistercian life is and should be. He tries to promote this life in Hauterive [in Switzerland], and I think he succeeds. Fortunately, till now, Hauterive has continued to be a small monastery. The danger for spiritual enterprises is always prosperity. Is the union of O.C.R. [Order of Reformed Cistercians, or Trappists] and S.O.C. a utopian dream? I would like to think not. But this re-union of Brothers, who have sometimes been and sometimes remain fence-Brothers, must be prepared by prayer and study in an atmosphere of search for Cistercian truth, and in an atmosphere of peace.

I pray for you, your monastery, and the whole Cistercian Order (I cannot break the unity, so strong in the Carta Caritatis; psychologically I have never accepted the schism of the beginning of the nineteenth century . . .). Pardon me the liberty of speech I take with you, and be sure that I am very faithfully yours in Our Lord and Our Lady.

Excuse too my awful English, but my writing is so bad that it is easier for you to read me in English than in French.

The opening lines indicate a missing letter of Merton to Leclercq, which dealt with the monastic approach to reading and meditating on the sacred Scriptures. Lectio divina *(or sacred reading) for the monk was the preamble to contemplative meditation on the Word of God, something which both Leclercq and Merton stressed in their writings. It should be noted that now Merton begins to confide in Leclercq his yearnings for a more eremitical life.*

Brussels

July 29, 1950

Returned in Brussels by the strike, I at last find time to answer your long and interesting letter of June 17.

I am glad you approve what I wrote about *lectio divina*. I do not think that we must try to settle an opposition between the spiritual and the scientific reading of the Scriptures: we must try to reconcile these two methods as was the case in the Middle Ages, when the same doctors explained the Bible using both methods. I tried to explain this in a paper to be published in the collection *Recontres* (Ed. du Cerf) about *L'Exégèse de l'Ancien Testament*:

1. In the Middle Ages there were two sorts of exegetics: scientific and spiritual;
2. But there were not two sorts of Scripture scholars: all used the two methods;
3. And these two methods of Scripture study supposed a same conception of Holy Scrip-

ture, and especially the relations between the Old and New Testaments.

I think that the way of teaching the Bible now common in our theological colleges is merely apologetic, which was probably very useful forty years ago. Now, thanks to a reaction against this apologetic reaction, we are finding the *media via* [middle way], the *via conciliationis non oppositionis* [way of reconciling what is not opposed]. One of the tasks of the monastic world today is to give a practical demonstration that this reconciliation is possible: we should not reject the results of modern biblical sciences, but nor should we be satisfied with them.

Probably by now you have seen that Gilbert of Stanford is not Gilbert of Hoyland: he is one of the many unknown spiritual writers who, though not all very original, show the intensity of the spiritual life in the monastic circles of the twelfth century . . .

I quite agree that the time is not ripe for a union (I avoid the word "fusion"; I prefer "union," which supposes distinction and differences: Distinguish in order to unite) between the S.O.C. and the O.C.R.* Some members of the S.O.C. are not sufficiently monks to

*The Cistercian Order currently is divided into two Orders: S.O.C. stands for the Sacred Order of Cistercians, more popularly known as the Cistercians of the Common Observance. O.C.R. (or O.C.S.O.) are the initials for the Order of Reformed Cistercians, known today as the Cistercians of Strict Observance, or simply the Trappists. There is a long-standing movement to unite the two Orders, but as of this writing (2001) it has not been achieved. The S.O.C. maintains schools and parishes in the United States, whereas the Trappists have remained strictly contemplative without an active ministry.

understand the O.C.R.; but I think that this union would be good for both Orders and should be prepared. Both parties should prepare an atmosphere of comprehension and sympathy, and the monastic element of the S.O.C. should come to have more influence. Dom [Matthaeus] Quatember is quite favorable to this monastic element. The next General Chapter of the S.O.C. in September will be of very great importance from this point of view. I think that some members of the S.O.C. have values of the spiritual and intellectual life which are quite in the Cistercian tradition.

Since I am preparing the edition of St. Bernard (and to start with, the *Sermones in Cantica*), I shall have to study his sources. If you have any information about his dependence on Origen, Gregory of Nyssa, and so on, you would be very kind to share it with me to help me in at least some orientations of my research. I feel the full weight of the difficulty of my work! And I am sometimes tempted to be discouraged. Everybody finds it natural to criticize, but there is no one who is willing to help.

I am not sufficiently acquainted with oriental mysticism to have an opinion of yoga and St. Bernard. But since all mystical experiences are fundamentally the same, there is surely some connection; and this not only in the experience itself, but also in the expression of it. From this point of view I think that depth psychology will shed some light on these profound and universal themes of the religious representation.

I do not know your *Spirit of Simplicity*, but I would be pleased to read it if ever I get the opportunity. I read recently the *Vie de Rancé* by Chateaubriand. It increased my desire to read Rancé.* I fear our judgments about him have been influenced by Chateaubriand and the romanticism of the monastic restorers of the last century. Whatever we may find excessive in Rancé is part of his times and is to be found also in Benedictines of the same generation; too much so for our liking. I fear that what we reprove in Rancé is dependent more on [Augustin] de Lestrange and other romantics.

I quite understand your aspiration to a solitary life. I think there has always been an eremitical tradition in the Cistercian and Benedictine Orders. In my opinion we are not to discuss personal vocations according to principles of community life, nor according to universal laws. We must always be very respectful of these vocations, provided they are real vocations and not illusions. Personally, though I am quite inapt for the eremitical life, I have always encouraged my confrères who aspire to such a life. Now, in France, there are some Benedictine monks who live as hermits in the mountains. Nobody knows it except God. The tradition of hermitages near monasteries or *inclusi* in monasteries seems very difficult to revive today. So we must find some new solutions to this problem. It is a

*Armand-Jean Le Bouthillier de Rancé (1626–1700) was the Abbot-reformer of La Trappe in France who stressed the penitential aspect of the monastic life. Merton and Leclercq were united in an effort to go beyond Rancé to the original charism of the twelfth-century Cistercians.

permanent problem and one which is a very good sign of the monastic fervor of the times: whenever cenobia are what they ought to be, they produce inevitably some eremitical vocations. The eremitical vocations disappear in times and countries where monasticism has ceased to be monastic.

Practically, now, the solution for such vocations is nearly always to move to an eremus, a charterhouse, or the eremi of the Camaldoli, that I know for sure.* Last year when I was in the eremus of Camaldoli, the master of novices was expecting an American Trappist. (I shall probably have to go again this year to the eremus at Frascati in order to study the writings of the founder.) The revival of the eremitical tendency in France has led to the inquiry being made by CHOC [Commission on the History of the Cistercian Order] about eremitical life. I can quite understand that your Abbot would like you to find a solution within the Cistercian life. Perhaps it is a providential occasion to restore reclusion. This is still practiced in Camaldoli. I saw that last year.

I would like to consult the book G. B. Burch, *The Steps of Humility* by Bernard, second ed., Cambridge, Mass., 1940. I cannot find it in Europe. Could you find it for me and either sell or lend it to me?

*The Camaldolese (O.S.B. Cam.) are a branch of the Benedictine Order founded by St. Romuald in the early eleventh century that allows for hermitages or individual cells for the monks, although the Brothers live more of a community style of monastic life. This is especially true of Frascati, which is in the hills outside Rome.

October 9, 1950

It is a long time since I received your July letter, which I read and pondered on with deep satisfaction. It is a privilege for which I am deeply grateful, to be able to seek nourishment and inspiration directly from those who keep themselves so close to the sources of monastic spirituality.

Your remarks on St. Bernard's ideas of Scripture are extremely important to me. I have been meditating on your Appendix to *Saint Bernard mystique*, and also I have been talking on this very subject to the students here. I agree with your conclusions about St. Bernard and yet I wonder if it would not be possible to say that he did consider himself in a very definite sense an exegete. My own subjective feeling is that the full seriousness of St. Bernard's attitude to Scripture is not brought out entirely unless we can in some sense treat him as an exegete and as a theologian, in his exposition of the Canticle. Naturally, he is not either of these things in a purely modern sense. But I think he is acting as a theologian according to the Greek Fathers' conception at least to some extent (see end of [Vladimir] Lossky's first chapter: *Theol. myst. de l'église orientale**). I think that is essentially what you were saying when you brought out the fact that he was seeking less to nourish his inte-

---

The Mystical Theology of the Eastern Church (London: James Clarke, 1957).

rior life than to exercise it. As if new meanings in his own life and Scripture spontaneously grew up to confirm each other as soon as Bernard immersed himself in the Sacred Text. Still, there is the evident desire of the saint to penetrate the Text with a certain mystical understanding and this means to arrive at a living contact with the Word hidden in the word. This would be tantamount to saying that for Bernard, both exegesis and theology found their fullest expression in a concrete mystical experience of God in His revelation. This positive hunger for "theology" in its very highest sense would be expressed in such a text as Can't. lxxiii, 2: "*Ego . . . in profundo sacri eloquii gremio spiritum mihi scrutabor et vitam*" [Deep in the bosom of the sacred word I shall search my spirit and my life]. He is seeking "*intellectum*" and "*Spiritus est qui vivificat: dat quippe intellectum. An non vita intellectus*" [The Spirit gives life: indeed he gives understanding. And is not understanding life?]. As you have so rightly said (p. 488), "*Sa lecture de l'E. Ste prépare et occasionne son expérience du divin*" [His reading of Scripture prepares and occasions his experience of the divine]. But I wonder if he did not think of Scripture as a kind of *cause* of that experience, and in some sense, "*servata proportione*" [keeping due proportion], as a Sacrament is a cause of grace? Scripture puts him in direct contact with the Holy Spirit who infuses mystical grace, rather than awakening in his soul the awareness that the Holy Spirit who infuses mystical grace has already infused a grace to that spoken of in Scripture. Or am I wrong? In any case, words like *"scrutabor"* [I shall search] and *"intellectus"* [understanding] tempt me to say (while agreeing in substance with all your conclusions) that there must have been a sense in which St. Bernard looked upon himself both as an exegete and as a theologian in his exposition of the Canticle. Although I readily admit there can be no question of his attempting as a modern author might to "make the text clear" or to "explain its meaning." That hardly concerned him, as you have shown. But do you not think that in giving the fruit of his own contacts with the Word through Scripture he was in a sense introducing his monks to a certain mystical "attitude" toward the Scriptures—not a method, but an "atmosphere" in which Scripture could become the meeting place of the Soul and the Word through the action of the Holy Spirit?

Perhaps these are useless subtleties: but you guess that I am simply exercising my own thought in order to confront it with the reactions of an expert and this will be the greatest service to me in the work that has been planned for me by Providence. I am also very much interested in the question of St. Bernard's attitude toward "learning," and feel that a distinction has not yet been sufficiently clearly made between his explicit reproofs of *"scientia"* in the sense of *philosophia* and his implicit support of *"scientia"* in the sense of *theologia*, in his tracts on Grace, Baptism, and his attacks on Abelard, not to mention (with all due respect to your conclusions) his attitude to the Canticle which makes that commentary also "*scientia*" [knowledge] as well as "*sapientia*" [wisdom]. Have you any particular lights on this distinction between science and wisdom in the Cistercians, or do you know of anything published in their regard? It seems to me to be an interesting point, especially to those of us who, like yourself and me, are monks engaged in a sort of "*scientia*" along with their contemplation! (It is very interesting in William of Saint-Thierry.)

I wish I could give you some information on St. Bernard in his relation to the Greek Fathers. I have none of my own; the topic interests me but I have barely begun to do anything about it, since I know the Greek Fathers so poorly. However, I can tell you this much: in [Jean] Danielou's *Platonisme et T. M.* on pages 7 and 211 there are references to St. Bernard's dependence (?) on St. Gregory of Nyssa. The opening of St. Bernard's series of *Sermons* so obviously reflects the idea of Origen and Gregory of Nyssa that the Canticle of Canticles was for the formation of mystics while Proverbs and Ecclesiastes applied to the beginners and progressives. I find Bernard's echo of this point an interesting piece of evidence that he considered the monastic vocation a remote call to mystical union—if not a proximate one. Then, too, Gregory's homilies on the Canticle of Canticles are full of a tripartite division of souls into slaves, mercenaries, and spouses. Gregory's apophatism is not found in St. Bernard, but in his positive treatment of theology Bernard follows Origen. I think Fr. Danielou also told me that Bernard's attitude toward the incarnate Word is founded on Origen—I mean his thoughts on *amor carnalis* [carnal love of Christ] in relation to mystical experience. I may be wrong.

A copy of *The Spirit of Simplicity* was mailed to you, but my own contribution to that work is confused and weak, I believe. I refer to the second part.

I agree with what you say about Abbé de Rancé and feel that my own treatment of him in *Waters of Siloe* had something in it of caricature. It is certainly true that Abbé de Lestrange was much more austere than Rancé.* To my mind the most regrettable thing about both of them was their exaggeration of externals, their ponderous emphasis on "exercises" and things to be done. Nevertheless, perhaps that is a sign of my own tepidity. It is true that the monastic life does demand faithful observance of many little exterior points of the Rule. These can certainly not be neglected *en masse* without spiritual harm. But one sometimes feels that for the old Trappists they were absolutely everything.

The Desert Fathers interest me much. They seem to have summed up almost everything that is good and bad in subsequent monastic history (except for the abuses of decadent monasticism), I mean everything that is good or bad in various monastic *ideals*.

---

*Augustin de Lestrange (1754–1827), last master of novices at La Trappe at the time of the French Revolution, gathered twenty-one monks of his community and fled to Switzerland, where he introduced even greater mortifications and penitential exercises than Rancé's community practiced at La Trappe.

Your news of the *De institutione inclusarum* [Instruction for recluses]—which you tell me with such detachment—is sad indeed. Do not think that manuscripts are only lost in Italy. A volume of our poems was printed by a man whose shop was in the country. Goats used to wander in to the press and eat the author's copy. This fortunately did not happen to our poems. Perhaps the goats were wise. They sensed the possibility of poisoning.

I am extremely eager to get Fr. [Louis] Bouyer's new book on monasticism, but have not yet been able to do so. I liked his *Saint Antoine*. Still, I wonder if he does not overdo his interest in the fact that in the early ages of the Church people were so clearly aware that the fall had put the devil in charge of material things. Fr. Danielou's *Signe du temple*, in its first chapter, gives a good counterpoise to that view—for heaven still shone through creation and God was very familiar with men in Genesis!

The other day we mailed Burch's *Steps of Humility* to you and it should be in your hands shortly. If you wish to send us something in return we would like to get [André] Wilmart's *Pensées du B. Guigue*, if this is Guigo the Carthusian. I have never yet gone into him. His lapidary style fascinates me. He is better than Pascal. Yet I love Pascal.

Your page on the eremitical vocation was very welcome. Someone told me the Carthusians were at last coming to America. I know the Trappist who has gone to Camaldoli. He was with me in the novitiate here. I wonder if he is happy there. His departure surprised me and I think his arrival surprised some of the Camaldolese.

Cistercian monasticism in America is of a genus all its own. Imagine that we now have one hundred and fifty novices at Gethsemani. This is fantastic. Many of them are sleeping in a tent in the quadrangle. The nucleus of seniors is a small, bewildered group of men who remember the iron rule of Dom Edmond Obrecht and have given up trying to comprehend what has happened to Gethsemani. The house has a very vital and enthusiastic (in the good sense) and youthful air like the camp of an army preparing for an easy and victorious war. Those of us who have been sobered by a few years of the life find ourselves in turns comforted and depressed by the multitude of our young companions of two and three months' standing: comforted by their fervor and joy and simplicity, and depressed by the sheer weight of numbers. The cloister is as crowded as a Paris street.

On the whole, when the house is completely full of men who are happy because they have not yet had a chance to suffer anything (although they believe themselves willing), the effect is a little disquieting. One feels more solidly rooted in God in a community of veterans, even though many of them may be morose. However, I do not waste my time seeking consolation in the community or avoiding its opposite. There is too little time for these accidentals.

I close this long letter thanking you again for yours, which are always so full of interest and profit.

Pray for me in my turn to be more and more a child

of St. Benedict—and if it be God's will, that I may someday find a way to be something of an eremitical son of St. Benedict! What of these Benedictines in the mountains of France? Have you more information about them? I am not inquiring in a spirit of restlessness! Their project is something I admire on its own merits.

Paris

October 26, 1950

Of course, I agree that St. Bernard was a theologian in the traditional sense of the word: *loqui Deo de Deo* [to speak to God about God]. This meaning has been preserved in the monastic tradition, and I explained that in my *Jean de Fécamp* [Joannes, Abbot of Fécamp, 995–1078/9]. I am coming to notice more and more how much not only St. Bernard but the whole monastic world of the twelfth century, Cistercian and Benedictine, is full of Origen. I gave a lecture on this subject three weeks ago at Chevetogne [French Benedictine abbey], and I have been asked to publish it in *Irenikon*. In it I pointed out this relation between the Greek Fathers and medieval monasticism. I had already dealt with the question in a very general way in 1945. Now I see things better. Maybe I shall collect everything I find on the matter and write a little article. The works of Origen which have been the most read by monks are his commentaries on Holy Scripture. And it is his exegesis, more than his doctrine, which influenced monks and Bernard.

Your distinction between *scientia* and *sapientia* is quite exact. It is a very traditional distinction, which obliged Thomas [Aquinas] in the *In quaestio* also to treat *theologia* as *sapientia*, although in another meaning of *sapientia*. For him

> *sapientia* is *cognitio per altissimas causas* [knowledge through the highest causes];
> *scientia* is *cogniti per causas immediatias* [a more certain knowledge achieved through immediate causes].

For tradition, poets, and monks, and in the Franciscan school,

> *scientia* is *cognitio per intellectum* [knowledge through the intellect];
> *sapientia* is "*scientia sapida*": *recta sapere* [wisdom is science rightly tasted].

It is this savor, *gustus*, which we find so frequently in Bernard, William of Saint-Thierry, and all other monks.

Another distinction which we often find in monastic literature is that between *scientia: cognitio intellectualis* [and] *conscientia: cognitio ad vitam* [science: an intellectual knowing (and) conscience: an awareness of the knowledge of life].

After further information, I now think that Rancé was no Cistercian at all. So you were quite right in what you said in *Waters of Siloe*.

I am now working on the unprinted writings of Gaufridus Antissiodorensis (=Altacomba=Claravallensis): a very good witness of the second generation of Cistercians and of St. Bernard. He insists constantly on discretion. I shall publish the more significant texts.

Fr. Bouyer's new book has not come out yet. It will surely interest you.

I hope I shall find Burch in Clervaux next week. I will send you the *Pensées* of Guigue, who is really Guigo the Carthusian. A nice book.

About the eremitical vocation: it is clear that the Cistercian vocation and life are, in themselves, eremitical. So a Cistercian normally should not have to seek this anywhere else than in his enclosure. The Cistercian's solitude depends on his silence. But it may happen that for accidental and psychological reasons—for example, if there are too many monks in the same monastery or if a monk has too much to do—he longs for more silence. Then I think that the solution for him is to change his monastery and seek silence and quiet elsewhere, in another Cistercian monastery.

My confrères in the mountains of Vercors are not making any noise. So I think all is well with them.

All best wishes, Father. Please pray for me. Next week I am going to Germany in search of Bernard's manuscripts.

Under obedience to his Abbot, Merton wrote a book on St. Bernard that was actually an introduction and commentary on the encyclical letter of Pope Pius XII called Doctor Mellifluus *and was appropriately titled* The Last of the Fathers. *It was translated into French and appeared in a series on monastic tradition that Leclercq and his Abbot, Jacques Winandy, were directing.*

Paris

June 17, 1952

Thank you very much indeed for your last letter and for *The Last of the Fathers.* Dom [Jacques] Winandy accepts it for his collection Tradition Monastique. I am glad also to have it. The publisher of the collection is pleased, too. I sent the volume to be translated, and we hope that it will be published toward autumn. I told the publisher, Mr. Wittmann, that you had instructed your agent to let us have the book on a "poor" basis.

Clervaux

March 17, 1953

It was very kind of you indeed to send your *Sign of Jonas*; thank you sincerely. I will try to answer you in my bad English, but most of us Frenchmen still write with a pen, as in the Middle Ages, and it takes me longer to write, even in French, with the typewriter. And I am not in the excellent condition [Antonin Gilbert] Sertillanges requires for intellectual life: about every five minutes the bell rings and I have to go to choir—with joy—or to wash dishes—also with joy—or something else.

As you are accustomed to receiving praise, I shall not send you one more letter of that sort. I will just say that I surveyed your book and I liked it. I think that I shall read it when I find time. It is written with this kind of freshness, a little "primitive," that we like in Americans (I suppose you permit me to speak to you simply, as a monk to another monk). I think this book, with *Seeds of Contemplation*, is exactly the kind of book you are made to write.

I've got an idea. Maybe you have heard of the little collection Tradition Monastique in which appeared the wonderful book by Bouyer, *Le Sens de la vie monastique*? I am one of the directors. Maybe it would be possible to publish a translation of your *Journal* or parts of it. Would you agree (since I see that your abbey keeps the copyright) to reserve for us the possibility of publishing a French translation in this collection? It does not depend only on me. But if you give me your agreement on principle, I will get in touch with the publisher, etc.

I am ashamed to say but I must confess that I did not read *The Seven Storey Mountain*. I didn't find time. But I know that my confrères like the book, and *Seeds* as well. I suppose that you are aware of the criticism made in Europe, especially in England, of your *Ascent to Truth*, and even in France, coming from the pen of Fr. [Louis] Bouyer in *Vie Spirituelle*. But these are the sorts of criticisms that Europeans are prepared to make. And the Church is everywhere, in the Old and the New World. In Europe we are so complicated: textual criticism has come to have such importance. We cannot even quote the *Pater noster* without putting a reference in the footnotes.

Let me tell you this: I am charged with organizing a congress on the theology of St. Bernard, and I invited a Cistercian of the Common Observance, whom I know to be a Doctor of Theology and, nevertheless, a very good monk. But recently, after many months, he wrote to say that he could not accept to come because, being in charge of the monastery hens and other things as well, in addition to choir, chapter, and so on, he had not found time to prepare a communication. On the other hand, I know several Trappists who are in pretty good condition for intellectual work. It is a sin against the motto of your Order: Una caritate. There seem to be two charities: one for the Trappists and another for the Common Observance. I think that the fault lies not only (maybe not chiefly) with you, but with your censors. And since your books, even in English, are expected to be read in Europe, I would suggest that one of the censors be European. There are some points of view that a European would feel. You remember the difficulties with the French translation of *The Waters of Siloe*, and the trouble this gave P. [Anselme] Dimier.

Of course, I understand that you are quite persuaded that the Trappist life is a very high state of perfection, and you are doing good apologetic work for it; but you must not forget that it is not the only form of contemplative life, at least in Europe.

Excuse me for all this. I give you an occasion for "*goûter les humiliations*" [tasting humiliations]. But you know that I do so because I esteem you and your life, and because I am very sincerely yours in the charity of Christ . . .

THOMAS MERTON TO JEAN LECLERCQ

May 18, 1953

Forgive me for my delay in answering your good letter. *Jonas* is already being translated for Albin Michel, so I regretfully decline your kind offer. It would have been an honor to appear in Tradition Monastique, in which series I already know your volume and that of Père Bouyer. By the way, has the promised [Odo] Casel volume appeared in this series yet? I am anxious to see it.

The remark about the monks of the Common Observance understanding the truth of a statement of Sertillanges on the intellectual life which Trappists are incapable of understanding does not seem to me to be an injustice. The statement of Sertillanges is true, and there is no injustice in saying that someone agrees with the truth. Nor was it intended to be disparaging. However, if it appears so to you, perhaps they will themselves be even more sensitive about it, so I will delete it from the French edition, along with a lot of other things which will be of no interest in France. One of the censors of *Jonas* was a European. Then, too, I think the book shows clearly that I do not consider the Trappist life the highest form of contemplative life, because I believe such a theory to be plainly false. The Trappist life is a solidly austere form of the monastic life, which has its limitations, which offers opportunities for a man to become a contemplative, provided the opportunities are not ruined by excessive activity within the monastery. We have something of the spirit of St. Bernard but we have no monopoly on it. From the little I know of Hauterive, I am certain they are just as good a monastery and just as proper for the contemplative life as Gethsemani—with perhaps certain advantages over Gethsemani. I do not despise the Common Observance at all, nor do I despise the Benedictines (as Dom Aelred Graham* seems to think).

The more I reflect on it, the more I realize that all the monastic ways to God are most worthy of praise, and that, in the end, there is no point in asking who has the most perfect interpretation of the Rule of St. Bene-

---

*Dom Aelred Graham, O.S.B., wrote a scathing attack on Merton that was published in *The Atlantic Monthly* ("Thomas Merton: A Modern Man in Reverse," January 1953, pp. 70–74). Graham felt strongly that Merton's flight from the world as expressed in his earlier books was too negative in its tone, not sufficiently world-affirming as his later books would be. He also thought Merton stressed the ascetic or penitential side of the monastic life too much. Merton took note of the criticism, and when he wrote *New Seeds of Contemplation*, a revision of the earlier *Seeds of Contemplation*, he dropped much of the negative emphasis. Merton later wrote a favorable review of Graham's *Zen Catholicism* (May 1963). As a result of this they became friends, and later Graham was very helpful in making contacts for Merton as he prepared for his Asian pilgrimage in the fall of 1968.

dict. In the end, however, what I most personally and intimately feel about at least my own place in the framework of things is echoed by the remarkable articles of a certain "S" in *La Vie Spirituelle* of last October and again more recently. Do you happen to know who this "S" may be, and would there be some chance of finding him and writing him a letter? I also, by the way, enjoyed your article in *Rythmes du Monde* now reproduced in *Témoignages*. I hope more and more to withdraw from the field of professional writing—or at least to appear in it only as an occasional author of disjointed meditations. But I do earnestly beg your prayers that I may seek God with greater love, and that He may deign to open to us here in America the ways of solitude, within the framework of our monasticism. This, I think, is much more important than any books.

JEAN LECLERCQ TO THOMAS MERTON

Clervaux

May 29, 1953

I am sending you my little book *La dottrina del Beato Paolo Giustiniani*, which is about the eremitical life of the Camaldolese.* I recently went again to the her-

---

*Blessed Paul Giustiniani was born in Venice in 1476, a contemporary of Michelangelo. He joined the Camaldolese hermitage at Camaldoli in Italy, but later became a reformer of the Order, which became a separate Order known as the Camaldolese Hermits of Monte Corona, near Frascati, outside Rome. A hermitage in McConnelsville, Ohio, was later founded from Frascati.

mitage of Frascati while I was in Rome, from which I have just got back. There is a real contemplative life there. It is not prosperity and numbers, but peace and prayer.

I appreciated your Preface to *St. Bernard* of CHOC.

I am glad that you are suppressing the allusion to Common Observance in the French translation of *Jonas*, and even I would like it to be deleted in the other translations and re-editions. I am not the only one who finds it regrettable, in spite of your good intention.

The author of the two beautiful articles on the eremitical life who signs "S" is Abbé J. Sainsaulieu. Of course you can write to him. The first article of *Vie Spirituelle*, October, is by my Abbot.

Yes, I pray for you because now, on account of your books, you have a responsibility which you must keep up. The news that you will no longer be a "professional writer" will please several people. You have done much good by your books, but you can also do so by the silence which you speak about. It is said that you can talk on the radio. But you have your vocation, of which no one is judge. Follow it.

THOMAS MERTON TO JEAN LECLERCQ

August 21, 1953

You must think me a very churlish and ungrateful person to leave your letter so long unanswered. We have had a busy summer, with much harvesting and other farm work. In addition to that our cow barn burned down and we have also bought a new farm, so that everyone has been exceptionally busy and I am two months behind with practically all correspondence.

Above all I want to thank you for your *Dottrina del B. P. Giustiniani*. I find it most useful and am glad to have it, particularly because it would otherwise be quite impossible for me to make the acquaintance of his personality and ideas. You have given us a valuable source. I hope books will appear on all the great Camaldolese figures. Dom [Anselmo] Giabbani sent me some pictures of Camaldoli and it is both beautiful and inspiring to me. I can well believe what you say about their having the true contemplative life at Frascati. I know nothing of that particular eremo. I would be interested in having some pictures of it, as I may perhaps do an article on the Camaldolese—by way of exception, since I do not write for magazines anymore. This would be in the hope of helping them make a foundation in this country. They are needed.

I find that in some monastic Orders there is a kind of selfish and dog-in-the-manger attitude toward other Orders and other forms of the contemplative life. One illusion that is very strong in this country still is the idea that the eremitical life is essentially "dangerous" and "impossible," etc. Some monks who claim to have a high contemplative ideal will actually run down the solitary life, and show a preference for the rather intense activity which is inevitable in a big, busy monastery of cenobites. It is all very well to have a big, busy monastery, but why claim that this is the highest possible ideal of contemplation! The French have a good word for that: *fumisterie* [a joke].

I am amused to think that I am supposed to be speaking on the radio. It is a great ordeal simply to speak to the monks in chapter. What would I do if I had to speak on the radio? I have not been out of the monastery for over a year, and then it was only for one day's journey. The only talk I have given outside the monastery was through the grille of the Louisville Carmel. I do not imagine that perfection consists merely in staying inside the enclosure, but the fact remains that I hate to go out and am very glad that I never have to do so. The last thing I would ever desire would be to speak on the radio.

Thank you for your prayers. I need them. And I hope they will obtain for me more and more solitude and obscurity and the humility proper to a true monk.

JEAN LECLERCQ TO THOMAS MERTON

In via pacis
September 23, 1953

I received your very good letter of August 21 just before leaving Clervaux for Dijon, where I had to play on the *theatrum mundi*, being the secretary of the theological congress on St. Bernard. This congress has been wonderfully interesting, much more than anyone ever expected. The lectures were all of a very high standard, from the double point of view of theology and spirituality (our chief trial is to reconcile them), and above all the atmosphere was always full of charity. Everybody was pleased and peaceful: discussion never became controversial; everything finished on Saturday afternoon with a very contemplative trip to Fontenay [a twelfth-century Cistercian monastery], where we all admired the style inspired by twelfth-century Cistercian life and "monastic theology." We had Fr. Jean Danielou, [Henri] de Lubac, [Jean] Mouroux, [Jean] Déchanet, [François] Rousseau, [Yves] Congar, Pacifique Delagaauw of Tilburg, Claude Botard of Orval, and others, all agreeing on the same themes of what they called "monastic theology," all coming to the conclusion that its characteristic is fidelity to patristic sources. They all said, too, that there is no opposition at all between "monastic" and "scholastic" theology, but the former could be useful to the latter. Professor A. Forest, a layman, but very contemplative, gave a very deep and beautiful lecture on St. Bernard and contemporary thought, in the style of his book, which I suppose you know, *La Vocation de l'esprit* (Paris, Aubier, 1953), each page of which could be illustrated with texts of St. Bernard. I will not tell you more about this congress: in a few months' time you will read, I hope, the text of all these lectures. Many of the Reverend Fathers at the General Chapter came from Cîteaux for two of the sessions. One Sunday morning, at Fontaines, in the rain, I had a very short talk with your Reverend Father, whom I am very, very glad to have met. And now I am on my way back to Clervaux, where I shall be tonight.

I tell you confidentially that your Reverend Father asked me if I could go and preach a retreat at Gethsemani. Of course, I just made objections—and I think they were sincere—and especially I pointed out that I really do not think that I speak English fluently enough. Let's wait and see if God gives further signs of His will. But of course, if Providence arranges for me to be in the States for some time, I would be pleased not only of the opportunity of seeing Cistercian manuscripts over there, and of searching for others, but also of seeing you and your community.

I have no more postcards of the eremo of Frascati. But I wrote to my friend Dom Maurizio, who is master of novices there, and I asked him to send you some. I hope you will get them. It would be a great charity if you could do something to make the Camaldolese of Monte Corona better known in America. It is not a question of propaganda; the point is rather that people who have an eremitical vocation may have the chance of living it and of knowing about this religious Order.

JEAN LECLERCQ TO THOMAS MERTON

Clervaux

October 13, 1953

I am writing to ask you a service. But of course you are quite free to refuse and I shall well understand.

This is what it is about: the publication of the

French text of my little book about the doctrine of Blessed P. Giustiniani has been decided. The title will be something like this: *Seul avec Dieu: La Vie érémitique selon le B. P. Giustiniani* [*Alone with God: The Hermit Life According to the Blessed Paul Giustiniani*]. The book will appear in the collection Tradition Monastique. But the publisher is a little afraid because he thinks that the book will interest only the Camaldolese. What has persuaded him to publish the book is that it is written by a Benedictine who he knows has nothing of the Camaldolese vocation.

You were good enough to write that you appreciated the book. Could you write a few pages to preface it? I think that if both a Cistercian and a Benedictine agree in presenting a book of this sort, any hesitation on the part of the publisher and the public will disappear. It should be made clear that though such a doctrine, such a life, and in particular this form of contemplative life, is an ideal not to be aimed at by all, it is a good thing that it should not be forgotten by anyone: it must remain a sign, a witness in the Church of God and in the monastic Order as a whole. So I thought you could further our common ideal.

If you and your Reverend Father agree to my proposition, you could write these few (or many) pages in English and I would translate them into French.

Everything is going peacefully here and, as far as I hear, in all our monasteries. Our Father Abbot has just come back from the blessing of the Abbot of Fontgombault, a new foundation made by Solesmes. In the last century it was occupied by Trappists. The church, pure twelfth-century style, is wonderfully clear, beautiful, and peaceful. It is just the style for our life. Here also we have one such monastery, modern but very pure.

By way of a sort of compensation I am sending you a few pages I have written on St. Bernard in the review *Camaldoli*. I think that all religious Orders, chiefly monastic Orders, have a great deal to learn from one another.

THOMAS MERTON TO JEAN LECLERCQ

November 5, 1953

It was a satisfaction for me when Father Abbot gave me permission to write the Preface for your volume on Paul Giustiniani. The Preface is completed and is on the way to you by surface mail.* I was happy to write it, and happy to go over your book again. I feel that it is especially important that the true place of the solitary in the Church should be brought out at this time, when there are so many who despise contemplation and when even in the monastic Orders there is a tendency to go off the right road precisely because the values for which the solitary exists are not appreciated.

Regarding the material side of the question: may I

*Merton's Preface to Leclercq's volume on Paul Giustiniani *Alone with God* was included in the volume *Disputed Questions*, published by Farrar, Straus in 1960.

depend on you to get this Preface censored by the two censors of our Order for the French language? I do not know who they are, but Chimay could tell you. All other material questions in regard to what I write are dealt with by an agent and he will be in touch with Plon in due course.

I have been reading with great satisfaction Cardinal Schuster's little volume.* It has a very fine tone, and its simplicity and solidity make it attractive as well as useful. I like it very much and feel that it is doing me good. It makes me wonder if I might not ask Cardinal Schuster to write a Preface to the translation of a forthcoming book of mine on the Psalms. Does he know English? Could you let me know, and I will send him a copy if he does.

It would indeed be a great pleasure to receive you at Gethsemani and have you preach our retreat. I sincerely hope that Divine Providence will bring you to America and that we will have this satisfaction. I was glad to hear of the theological conferences at Dijon and look forward to seeing them in print.

Returning to Giustiniani—could the Camaldolese at Frascati perhaps send me a picture or a relic of him?

---

*Cardinal Ildefonso Schuster, although of Austrian-Bavarian parents, grew up a thorough Roman. He entered St. Paul-outside-the-Walls Benedictine Abbey in Rome as a monk and became a renowned liturgical and monastic historian. After being elected Abbot of his monastery, he was given many positions in the Vatican before his appointment as Archbishop of Milan in 1929. He later was named Cardinal and worked at the Vatican. *La Vie monastique dans la pensée de Saint Benoît* is the small book referred to by Merton, published by Plon in 1953.

Even some pictures of their eremo. I am still hoping to write a little something on the Camaldolese, to make them known in America. Any information or books they send will be useful to me and to their own cause.

I certainly agree wholeheartedly that the monastic Orders have much to learn from one another, and we in America have much to learn from you in Europe. We are very isolated and provincial, I am afraid, and our undue sense of our own importance may perhaps delude us that we are the only monks in the world. It may not be possible for me to satisfy the desires of my own heart, but at least I can continue to have zeal for God's truth and for the monastic ideal. Pray for me, and may we remain united in Christ and St. Benedict.

JEAN LECLERCQ TO THOMAS MERTON

November 23, 1953

I have received your letter, and then the Preface. I have read it and shall translate it. I think it is just what was necessary, and that will be useful for the book. May we be unanimous in the esteem for the contemplative life, even of the solitary life, even if we are unable to live according to this ideal. As regards the easier life of activity, it will never be necessary to speak of it to monks. The natural tendency, with very good reasons, is always going to the active life. But it is necessary to recall that solitude and contemplation are also legitimate in the Church of God.

The Prior of Scourmont tells me that the censors are now anonymous. So I shall send the translated Introduction to the Rev. Fr. General in Rome.

My friend Dom Maurizio, novice master of the eremo at Frascati, writes me that he has been delighted to see your Reverend Father at the eremo and that he gave him some pictures of the eremo. As regards relics of Blessed Giustiniani, I wonder if they have anything but the autographs. And there is no great literature on the subject. But I shall write to Dom Maurizio about that.

Yes, on the whole, the book of Cardinal Schuster is really a fine book. Some details seem to be nonsense, but the general impression, surely, is authentically Benedictine.

I suppose Cardinal Schuster would accept to write for you a Preface. He is very attached to everything which is monastic. I am going to Milan for a lecture at the Catholic University on St. Bernard, Theologian. He will speak the last day. I shall pay him a visit and ask him about your Preface. And I will answer you. I suppose he does read English.

Don't think at all that you Americans are monks of secondary quality. On the contrary, I think that you are, and for some time, in better condition than we are as regards *sancta simplicitas* [holy simplicity]. Here, in this old, too old, Europe, we all are sophisticated, intellectual, complicated; we are dying of erudition. We have no spontaneity anymore, nothing of the *spiritus liberatis* [liberty of spirit] which is necessary to any creation or renovation. There is in your monasticism something of ingenuousness that we are tempted to despise; but you are right. We know all the constitutions, statutes, texts, and so on, but we are quite unable to invent anything adapted to new times. That is why I hope so much from you in America, especially as regards intercommunion; if some revival is to come, it will come from you. You have more liberty of mind, and more courage. We may have more austerity, more science, more culture. But the sources of life are with you. I have not been alone; in Dijon last August, when we saw all the Trappists, one got the impression that the Americans reminded us of the first Cîteaux. In the first Cîteaux there was also this kind of freshness, of liberty, of initiative, of courage in the life, of which you have something. You are probably not very conscious of it, but I expect that your Abbots must feel it when they come over here. And even this "unawareness of your importance" of which you speak is a sign of vitality: you still believe in monastic life, you have the impression of having discovered it, it is a new reality for you. For us, it is an old, venerable institution which we try to preserve, like archaeologists do for museum pieces. Of course, we also believe in monastic life, but in more of an intellectual way. Also, the first Cistercians believed that they were the only monks. The old, too old, Benedictines protested. But it was true that the life had passed to the Cistercians. I, for instance, noticed from experience that you are more free from prejudices, more ready to accept history as it has been, than here in Europe. We always fear dangers for the uniformity, or for the reputation of the Order, or for our sentimental piety. You don't fear. You look forward to the future. Fear is proper to old people. And when we are too old, we die . . . We are not yet dying. But I am sure that we have at least as much to learn from you as you have from us. That's why everything that helps us to know your ways and methods is useful to us.

Excuse this long digression.

THOMAS MERTON TO JEAN LECLERCQ

December 7, 1953

What you say about our American monks having a true monastic spirit is gratifying. I cannot deny that the Holy Spirit is truly at work here. And there is much spontaneity. But I do not think we have any of the solidity of European monasticism, and in our fervor there is much that is merely human enthusiasm. Also much provincialism.

I believe it is good for me to work for the *monastic* ideal as a whole, and not be a "propagandist" for any one Order. Indeed, I think the more we work for unity among ourselves, the better it will be.

[P.S.] Are you doing anything special at Clervaux for the Marian Year?

Leclercq saw Cardinal Schuster and asked him about doing a Preface to Merton's volume Bread in the Wilderness. *The Cardinal, who had recently been appointed to a high Vatican position, said he was not at liberty to write one, because he was extremely busy with one of the Congregations in Rome.*

January 8, 1954

Many thanks for your translation of the Preface. I have read it with pleasure and satisfaction and am returning it to you with a few minor corrections. In one place I suppressed a couple of lines. I discovered since writing them that they are not in accord with the conception of the eremitical life favored by the Camaldolese of Monte Corona, who have no *coenobium* [community life]. I had not realized that. They are certainly in possession of the authentic tradition of St. Romuald on this point.

Thanks also for asking Cardinal Schuster for the Preface. I expected he would probably refuse. A copy of *Bread in the Wilderness* went to Dom Winandy from here. I asked the publishers to send you a review copy, but this will be delayed. The sale of the first edition was exceptionally large and they had not made provision for the immediate printing of a second. The book is printed on special paper.

Is the *Gallia eremitica* worth having? Do you know about how much it would cost?

I am teaching a course on the theology of St. Paul—

and I have [Lucien] Cerfaux, [Ernest Bernard] Allo, etc.
Do you know of anything especially good in the way of
new work on St. Paul? (I also have *Gnosis* by Jacques
Dupont.)

[P.S.] Our good Giustiniani calls the solitary life a life
"with Christ": What reading for solitaries is found in
St. Paul? Solitude then becomes a life in the fullest sense
in Xto, possessed by the Spirit of the Lord!

JEAN LECLERCQ TO THOMAS MERTON

Clervaux

April 7, 1954

I have just received your fine book *Bread in the Wilderness*. I thank you very much for having had the idea of
getting it sent to me by the editor. I am going to see
where I can review it; it is perhaps a bit late. Truth to
tell, I had already admired and glanced through this
book at Fr. Bruno Scott James's place and then here,
where I saw a copy you sent to my Father Abbot.

The editor of Tradition Monastique has just written
to us yesterday to say that the collection is not a good
commercial venture. Dom Winandy and I are not surprised. We did not aggressively publicize the series, so it
was not a success either. The volume on the doctrine of
Giustiniani will soon be in press and will come out in
the autumn. Then it is possible that the collection will
not be able to go on . . . The editor adds that it would

be good to have a best-seller title to get the collection on its feet. If ever one day you write something the "agent" would leave you free to publish in a poor collection, think of us . . . I do not know whether, there in America, you grasp what sort of books are usually published by Albin Michel; certainly it is not encumbered with piety. That is probably one of the reasons why it is successful and brings in money. But it would be a good thing if at least once you could write just for the glory of God, with no money involved. And that would have the advantage of reacting to a fairly widespread idea in Europe: T. Merton brings in money, so his Superiors exploit him as much as possible, because of the income. I think that is a wrong idea, and I say so every time I have a chance: but it would be a good thing for the practical demonstration to come for once from you and your Superiors.

Forgive me for saying frankly things that so many people think. Take it as a proof of friendship. And go on writing books which do good, since you have found a style which our contemporaries like.

As for me, I go on working. Erudition does not bring success, certainly; especially not commercial success. But the Benedictine life such as we have it in Europe still allows some of us to devote ourselves to it for the Church. Moreover, the more chances I have of seeing other forms of monastic life, the more I think that our European Benedictine life realizes a good balance, a real life of prayer . . .

April 27, 1954

I have just written to the agent. I suspect that Plon is unjustly penalizing you because the agent sought some kind of material settlement for the Preface. I had not stopped to think that this might happen. The only reason why I use an agent is quite obvious—it saves me an immense amount of correspondence, contract work, and business worries. If I did otherwise, I would never have any time for anything except business. I simply leave all cares to the middle-man. This of course has its hard-boiled aspects, since the agent is bent on making a living out of his percentage. I do not think it is altogether fair of Plon to retaliate by threatening the future of your series, although in a way I see where that is logical—with the logic of the jungle.

However, if it will help your series at all to publish a book by me, I have a small volume on St. Bernard about to appear. It is very slight, not a formal life, simply a brief introduction to the saint and to the recent Encyclical. It has three parts—a sketch of his life and character, an outline of his works and teaching, and a commentary on the Encyclical—followed by the text of the papal document itself. I had not even thought of allowing this book to be published in France. When you see it, you will probably agree that it adds nothing to the number of excellent studies of St. Bernard, including your own. I do not think it will help your series except accidentally. If the appearance of the author's name is of any use to you, I will consent to let this book appear in France—without worrying about what may happen to my reputation.

I can agree with what you say about the Benedictine life. The more I come into indirect contact with the Benedictine houses of Europe, like yours and La Pierre-qui-Vire, the more I appreciate the depth and solidity of the monastic spirit, and profit by contact with it. It is indeed a paradox that you do now in fact have much more real silence and peace than many a Trappist monastery. I never felt any sympathy with Rancé's ideas about erudition, and I am sure that the work done by Benedictines today in this field is perfectly monastic and truly fruitful in the line of monastic spirituality.

The last thing in the world a monk should seek or care about is material success. That which I see in my own labors is as much a surprise to me as it is to anybody else. Nor can I find in myself the power to get very interested in that success. I do not claim this to be a virtue, because I never really understood money anyway. I do not know how much our books have acquired. The figures are not communicated to me, and if they were I would probably not understand them anyway.

In any case I have instructed the agent to take some kind of cognizance of the problem you mention in your letter. It is of course inevitable that such things should be said about me, and I do not see what there is to be done about it. Thank you for defending the truth. Meanwhile, I have also told the agent that if you want the St. Bernard book, *The Last of the Fathers*, I would like you to have it on a "poor" basis.* That will at least give me satisfaction of cooperating in a work which I admire, for I have derived great pleasure and profit from reading the volumes that have reached me so far. It is quite certain that if the monastic life is to fulfil its important role in our world today, there must be books that reflect the peace and sanity and depth of the true monastic tradition. Not all monastic books fulfil that function, for in every part of the Church cockle can be intermixed with the good wheat.

Please do not feel yourself obliged to write a review of *Bread in the Wilderness*. My only way of getting a copy to you was to have the publisher send you a review copy. If, however, you do write a review, I shall feel very pleased and honored.

Please commend me to the prayers of your dear Lord Abbot and ask his blessing for me. Let us continue in union of prayers and in solitude, *in limine aeternitatis* [on the threshold of eternity].

JEAN LECLERCQ TO THOMAS MERTON

Clervaux
July 13, 1954

I understand your worries. I also understand the point of view of your Superiors. There is probably some rea-

*Merton, with his Abbot's approval, agreed to allow *The Last of the Fathers* to appear in French on a "poor" basis, in contrast to his usual practice with his French publishers, who worked through an agent.

son for them tightening up the censorship. There are things which Europeans do not yet easily understand . . . I remember last year when I was in Rome I heard some speak with displeasure about your *Journal*. Be this justified or not, it is understandable that Superiors should take this into consideration. For us, everything is all right, and it is so simple just to let people do as they like with us. But I realize that relations with a publisher are not for all that made more simple.

The prohibition of *The Last of the Fathers* would probably be the death sentence of our collection, and with the same blow Giustiniani will not be able to come out, as they were to be published together. So I hope the translation will be allowed. It is true that your book makes no very new contribution to history or to theology, but what you write is never insignificant. And then we have had a lot of big books about St. Bernard, but we still need a sketch giving an all-over view and a readable text of the Encyclical (there is a French translation of this, but only in reviews not read by the general public). So I still hope. About the translation, in fact it is almost finished, and by the time you receive this letter it will probably be entirely finished. We could of course give it to your translator, but is it reasonable to do again work which has been well done by one of our novices who did all his schooling at Downside and knows English as well as he does French? Furthermore, the text is short, not counting the Encyclical (of which we shall give the Vatican's official French translation) and the extracts from St. Bernard; it comes to about sixty pages. There is not much to be earned from this translation. We did it quickly because the editor wants the manuscript by the beginning of August so that it can come out in the autumn. Now I am in a bit of a fix. Moreover, the reason why we got one of us to translate it is to avoid paying a translator royalties, which would be a burden for this poor collection we are trying to save. Well, tell me what you think about all that.

THOMAS MERTON TO JEAN LECLERCQ

July 28, 1954

Yesterday I heard from our Reverendissime Père Abbot General and I hasten to let you know that he raises no objection to the publication of *The Last of the Fathers*. So you may proceed with it as fast as you like. Also, about the translation, that too is settled. It seems that Albin Michel had already advertised or announced *The Sign of Jonas* and it was not possible for the work to be stopped altogether. Consequently we have no need of any other work for Marie Tadié.* It is therefore to be published, but will be censored and abridged by our Abbot General himself and two censors. I don't expect that very much will remain after they get through with

*Marie Tadié had been the translator of some of Merton's works into French, but she was beginning to act more and more as an agent, not only for French but also for other European languages, until Merton (and the Abbey of Gethsemani) was forced to terminate her services. Merton had other publishers and translators in Spain, Portugal, Italy, and elsewhere and previous long-standing commitments.

it—the two covers, the Prologue, and the Epilogue, no doubt: with a few pages in between.

It is true that religious in Europe are not yet used to journals, but the secular reader in France certainly has begun to acquire a taste for them. Witness the success of the journals of Gide, Green, and Du Bos. I am glad my own journals will be expurgated, but in the long run it would seem to be not a bad idea that, for once, by way of exception, such a production should come from a monastery. I would give anything for a journal, even the most trivial, written in twelfth-century Clairvaux. But then, indeed, they did *not* keep journals.

There is just one thing about *The Last of the Fathers*. If I get time in the next ten days, I would like to write an extra page or two on the spirit of St. Bernard, perhaps also on his youth and early formation (which ought not to be completely passed over in silence even in a sketch), and perhaps on one other point. Please bear with me for a few days and leave space for the inclusion of these pages.

The thought that the publication of this book in your series will aid the appearance of the Giustiniani volume is one which gives me great satisfaction. I feel much more gratified about being a writer now that I see that I can help other authentic testimonies of the monastic spirit appear. I shall do everything I can to let you have another book, in order to help your series. Please tell your good Father Abbot that I feel that I am really doing the work of God in collaborating as much as I can with your series, and will feel that my own writing is thereby inserted in a truly monastic context. There is a special satisfaction in collaborating with one's brothers in Christ, and I do not like the idea of an isolated, and spectacular, apostolate. No doubt I must have the courage to face the enemies that this isolation makes for me—even among priests and religious. But for my own part I prefer to be a member of a team, at least to some extent, than to be a soloist exclusively. However, since God has singled me out for a kind of isolation I will certainly accept it, together with its consequences. That is certainly nothing new in the Church.

JEAN LECLERCQ TO THOMAS MERTON

Clervaux

August 30, 1954

Many thanks indeed for your new pages, which I enjoyed translating. I appreciated your mention of France: I dislike Frenchmen praising France, but I like it when it comes from abroad. That will make up for some words you have on France in *The Seven Storey Mountain*. I shall send these pages off today, and they will be inserted, so everything will be all right once more.

We have another American book which I hope we may be able to publish in French. It is *Holy Work* by Dom Rembert Sorg, O.S.B. Our novice-translator has found a very nice title: *La Prière des mains*; it deals with monks' manual labor. The book has its defects, but we would present it as an "essay" and add a selection of traditional monastic texts. Coming from an American Benedictine, this witness might find some echo in European Benedictine circles. On the other hand, the fact of being published in France will give it a little bit of prestige—so the author thinks—in some American Benedictine circles. So, once more we shall have helped one another. Let's not wait until the Russians oblige us to discover again that manual labor is compatible with monastic life. Let's begin before monasteries are transformed into kolkhozy. Did you hear about the recent monastic reform issued by the government itself in Bulgaria (I think)? It is a very interesting reform, based mainly on the Rule of St. Benedict, even though they are Orthodox, with the obligation of working as many hours a day as ordinary people do.

We are correcting the proofs of S. Bernard théologien. I think last year's Dijon lectures will be a very valuable contribution to the knowledge of St. Bernard's theology.

And in the meantime let's pray and live in peace; let's always be ready and free.

THOMAS MERTON TO JEAN LECLERCQ

November 4, 1954
It was good to receive the good news in your last letter. I will look forward to seeing the St. Bernard book. No copy has as yet arrived. However, will you ask Plon to

send me another dozen copies of it? And what about your Giustiniani? That was supposed to appear at the same time. Is it out yet? I am almost more interested in it than in *The Last of the Fathers*. A book about solitude is closer to my heart.

I am glad the new edition of St. Bernard is finally under way. I shall pray for you and your co-workers. It is a great and important task, even though it may not attract much public attention. And it is a most monastic enterprise. God will surely bless it, and you. And the rest of us will benefit greatly. When do you think the complete edition will be ready? I will probably make this an excuse for delaying work in my book on St. Bernard, which, incidentally, I have never even begun. There are so many other things to be done—and beyond all that is the monastic life itself, which does not consist in "doing" anything, but in being a perfect son of God, and tasting the joy of the *paradisus claustralis* [paradise of the cloister]. I am asking my agent to see that all other foreign translations of *The Last of the Fathers* are made from the French edition.

JEAN LECLERCQ TO THOMAS MERTON

Clervaux
November 17, 1954
Feast of St. Gertrude

Dom Gabriel [Sortais] paid us a short visit last week. We were very glad.

I am correcting the galley proofs of Giustiniani, which, I think, will come out in about a fortnight. Copies will be sent to you immediately. Reading it again in proofs, I realize that it contains many very nice texts. It is a pity, in a way, that it deals with "hermits"; this single word will make some people think that it is for solitaries only. Whereas, actually, they are suitable for many cenobites. Your Preface will help to show that up.

I think the complete edition of St. Bernard will be finished in nine years . . . if everything goes well . . . But what a job! How anxious I am sometimes, often, about the authentic recension and so on . . . But that's my job in the Church of God. I must accept it.

The annual retreat is now on. A Carmelite Father is talking to us about holy hope. Very beautiful doctrine, not at all pessimistic. I like that.

THOMAS MERTON TO JEAN LECLERCQ

April 27, 1955

Our Regular Visitation was finished just a few days ago, during which the Visiting Abbot concentrated his attention on what he called "a hermit mentality" in the monastery. He strongly disapproved of it, although recognizing in a private conversation that on my side I had a particular spirit, that I did not enter into "the pattern," and that he did not really expect to see much change in me. But altogether, we have reached a point at which I think that I cannot, or even should, remain at Gethsemani, or in the Cistercian Order. There is truly no place for me here, and altogether I am very glad that the Regular Visitation has swept away the little ineffectual compromises which my Father Abbot had thought up in order to "arrange matters."

They are willing to receive me at Camaldoli d'Arezzo. I have a friend who is willing to pay my steamer fare. I have even made a vow myself to pass to a "solitary and contemplative" life (something about which I have thought for a long time). Well, there remains an enormous obstacle: my own Superiors. I believe that my Father Abbot will try to hold me back at all costs. I am going to ask him not only permission to go to Camaldoli (which he will refuse peremptorily). I will tell him again of my intention to write to the Congregation [of Religious] to ask for a transitus,* provided that he does not oppose this in advance so as to block everything. But it really seems to me that because they more or less recognize in the Order that I have an eremitical spirit, it would be unreasonable to insist that I stay here after this spirit has been officially disapproved. I do not know what is going to happen. Only I ask you this: could you answer the following questions for me:

1. Is it true that they do not truly live a contemplative life at Camaldoli, that "silence is

---

* "Transitus" is a term for official permission to transfer from one monastic Order to another. Such a transfer for a monk in solemn vows requires permission from the Sacred Congregation of Religious in Rome. In Merton's case it would have been a transitus from the Trappists to the Camaldolese, a branch of the Benedictines that allows more solitude for its individual members.

poorly observed," that the Prior entirely disposes of the hermits' vocations, that he can send them back to the cenobium against their will, at his own pleasure? (These are the things they tell me to make me give up my idea of going there.)

2. Can the vow to pass to a more solitary and contemplative life be made by a Benedictine monk, or is this incompatible with our vow of stability?

3. Do you think it would be better to go to Camaldoli or to Frascati? I am thinking of Camaldoli because Dom Giabbani wants soon to make a foundation in America, and I am in touch with him.

4. If I cannot go to Camaldoli or Frascati, could you tell me where I could find an analogous eremitical life, apart from the Charterhouse?

5. If I go to Camaldoli I am a little afraid of being exploited as a celebrity. Do you think that there is a real danger of that? If so, how can I escape it?

6. Is there a way of submitting an application for transfer in such a way that it would be accepted even if the Superior of the house is against it?

In fine, I do all this believing that God wants it of me. I really believe that the time has come for me to *have* to do something for myself, for nobody here is going to do it for me. It is evident that my Superiors are themselves not going to do anything to smooth the way for me to become a hermit. I am doing everything with a good deal of peace, with the same feelings that accompanied my entry into the Church—with the sensation of having my hand in the hands of God. I do not know where this is going to end, but I ask you above all to pray for me.

I have written this in French so that your dear Rev. Father Abbot also may read it. He may have a word of advice to give me because he is in favor of eremitical vocations. He doubtless knows how much must be suffered in order to open the way to the desert. I ask him and you also to bless me. Above all, pray. I shall be very happy to receive your advice. If you want to talk this over with Dom Maurizio, I would be pleased. Let them at Frascati also pray for me. I would like to join our ex-Brother Brendan there. If one could believe that they will make an American foundation, I would rather go there than to Camaldoli. But having spoken of this to Dom Maurizio, I ask you not to tell any others.

So there, my dear Father. I am glad at having friends who can help me. Here I have a director who is favorable to this change, but he is leaving soon to make a foundation.

Believe me ever united to all of you in the silence of God. And your Giustiniani, when will he appear?*

*This book on the life and doctrine of Paul Giustiniani by Jean Leclercq was first published in French with a Preface by Thomas Merton in 1955. It was later translated and published in the United States by Farrar, Straus under the title *Alone with God* in 1961.

The missing letter referred to in the first sentence dealt with Merton's vocational crisis. Having consulted Dom Verner Moore of Sky Farm (Carthusian foundation in Vermont), he decided to try entering the Camaldolese in Italy. His Abbot, Dom James, was opposed to this plan as well as to a move in the direction of the Carthusians.

June 3, 1955

Many thanks for your letter of May 26. I wish I had received it sooner. Early in May, having consulted the Carthusian Father Dom Verner Moore at Sky Farm, I received from him a very positive encouragement to transfer to Camaldoli and my director here thought I should follow this suggestion, so I applied for a transitus. So far nothing has been heard from Italy, however, and Father Abbot is very much opposed to my going to Camaldoli, and I suppose his objections may lead to the refusal of the transitus, although the Abbot General says he feels that if it is the will of God he sees no reason for my not going. Things are still in a fluid state, however, and with Father Abbot I am earnestly trying to reach the final solution. One thing is certain, everyone more and more seems to agree that I should not stay in the precise situation in which I find myself at the moment. I honestly believe, and so do my directors, that being a cenobite is no longer the thing I need. However, I have no desire to become a preacher of retreats at Camaldoli either, still less an exploited celebrity, although I do feel that even then I would have far more solitude and silence there than I have here. I may be wrong.

However, Dom James is very interested in the question, and he has even proposed to place before higher Superiors the possibility of my becoming a hermit in the forest here. If this permission were ever granted it would solve all my problems, I think. The forest here is very lonely and quiet and covers about a thousand acres, and there is much woodland adjoining it. It is as wild as any country that would be found in the Ardennes or the Vosges, perhaps wilder. I could be a hermit without leaving the land of the monastery. One could begin the project gradually and imperceptibly, for the government is putting up a fire-observation tower on one of our hills and the future hermitage could be in connection with this—one could begin simply by being the watchman on the tower and gradually take up permanent residence there. Unfortunately, the higher Superiors, as far as I can see, are absolutely closed to any such suggestion and even refuse to permit a monk to work alone on the observation tower. Dom James is placing the matter before the Abbot General.

Apart from this the best suggestion seems to be that I should secretly enter a hermitage of Monte Corona, and live there unknown without writing or publication, as a true solitary. Dom James is not fully in favor of this, but he has given me permission to write and inquire about it. I have written to Dom Maurizio. Dom James does not want me to leave the Order, mainly because of the comment that would be excited among souls. I think, however, that I could leave secretly enough to keep that comment at a minimum. It would never be more than a rumor, and there have been so many rumors before that people would not pay much attention, until it was all forgotten.

I am waiting still to hear from your Father Abbot. I will value his suggestions. Meanwhile, the main purpose of this letter is to ask about the hermit who lives fifty miles from Clairvaux. How does he live? Does he entirely support himself? Does he receive any aid from the monastery? Does he have any contact with seculars? How does he say Mass, if he is a priest? Tentatively we are planning here a life in which food could be brought to me from the monastery in the seasons in which I could not grow enough for myself—bread, rice, and so forth. It would not be necessary to go to the Bishop, would it, since I would be living on the monastery's land?

I was interested to hear there was a hermit at La Trappe under Rancé. I value your prayers in this time of mystery and searching. It is more and more evident to me that someone must go through this kind of thing. By the mercy of God, I am one of those who must pass through the cloud and the sea. May I be one of those who also reach the Promised Land. Whatever happens, I shall certainly write much less as I have no desire to become a "literary hermit." I feel that God wills this solitude in American monasticism, even if someone has to leave America temporarily to find it.

THOMAS MERTON TO JEAN LECLERCQ

August 11, 1955

I am sending this together with a note to your good Reverend Father to thank him for writing to me about his hermit. He certainly seems to have a very good situation, and I envy him. If I ever manage to become a hermit here the difficulties will be much greater, but that is nothing special. The very idea of the solitary life is to live in direct dependence on God, and in constant awareness of our own poverty and weakness.

I have also received a letter from Frascati in which they say they will be quite willing to receive me to make a trial of their life, incognito. I could remain with them without being a writer, in true obscurity and solitude. My Superiors do not wish to give me permission to make this trial, as far as I can see at the moment, but I should very much like to visit Frascati and other places where the eremitical life is led. Here again I must rest in my poverty and let God provide.

At the moment, it does seem that there is a real chance of my being allowed to live in solitude here. Higher Superiors have softened their rigid opposition to some extent, at least admitting the eremitical solution in theory. But Dom James, my Father Abbot, is showing himself more and more favorable to the idea, and I believe that insofar as it may depend on him, I can hope for this permission. Meanwhile on the material side, the way seems to be preparing itself. The State Forestry Department is erecting a fire-lookout tower on one of our big hills, a steep wooded eminence in our forest, dominating the valley by about four hundred feet. I have been put in charge of this work with them, and they are going to erect a small cabin there, in which one might conceivably live. It will be an austere and primitive kind of hermitage, if I ever get to live in it. In any case I depend on your prayers, and those of all who are interested in helping me, that Our Lord may be good to me, and if it be His will that I may live alone in our forest. In the meantime I think I can count on a semi-solitary life for part of the year as the watchman on this fire tower. That will be beautiful—unless it is disapproved by higher Superiors. But they have seemingly permitted it as an experiment. Again, I beg your prayers.

I have stopped writing, and that is a big relief. I intend to renounce it for good if I can live in solitude. I realize that I have perhaps suffered more than I knew from this "writing career." Writing is deep in my nature, and I cannot deceive myself that it will be very easy for me to do without it. At least I can get along without the public and without my reputation! Those are not essentially connected with the writing instinct. But the whole business tends to corrupt the purity of one's spirit of faith. It obscures the clarity of one's view of God and of divine things. It vitiates one's sense of spiritual reality, for as long as one imagines himself to be accomplishing something he tends to become rich in his own eyes. But we must be poor, and live by God alone—whether we write or whatever else we may do. The time has come for me to enter more deeply into that poverty.

The main purpose of this letter is this: I am cleaning out my files. There is one manuscript which I think ought to interest you for your Tradition Monastique. It is a short, simple collection of meditations on solitude which I wrote two years ago, when I had a kind of hermitage near the monastery. I still have it, but it is no longer quiet. Machines are always working near it, and there is a perpetual noise. Nobody uses it very much, except on feast days. But at any rate these pages on solitude are perhaps worth sending to you. They will make a small volume, better I think than *Seeds of Contemplation* and more unified. Tentatively I am calling it simply "Solitude" [published later as *Thoughts in Solitude*].

The manuscript is being typed. Let me know if you are interested, and when it is finished I shall be sending it to you.

I look forward with great interest to your study on the eremitical life. I recently re-read your pages on the hermits of Cluny, and wonder if you ever published the article on Peter the Venerable and hermits, which you spoke of some time ago. I should like an offprint if you did.

Finally, I am still hoping to hear some news of the Giustiniani book.

68

I am glad that Our Lord is slowly and mysteriously opening out a new way before me. I am glad too that you have been in the mystery, and have contributed something to its working out. I trust you will stay with me by your prayers, and on occasion by your good advice. My chief reaction is a deep understanding of my poverty, and a feeling of solitude which is a kind of lack of human support (there is in fact some opposition on the part of some in the monastery to this "solitary" tendency). True, one must go without support, one must learn to walk on water. But I like to think the Church is supporting me nevertheless, and that I am not merely wandering off on my own tangent. There are never lacking souls who tell everyone who tries to be a hermit that the solitary life is a temptation of the devil. I know I must have the faith to go forward in spite of this accidental opposition, once I have the encouragement of directors, Superiors, and friends: all the same, it is not easy for me. Pray that I may learn to follow Christ.

THOMAS MERTON TO JEAN LECLERCQ

September 25, 1955

Here is the manuscript which I spoke of—let us say that about half of it is on solitude. I am afraid of being too open about the nature of the book, as it is not thought to be desirable for me to appear too much as a solitary. There is enough general material in this to make it something else than a tract on solitude.

Whether or not it will be an immense success in your collection I have no idea. Perhaps you will believe me if I tell you that I am not the least interested in literary success and never have been—at least not since entering the monastery—and I certainly cannot say that this material was written with any thought of literary success. In fact, if you ask my frank opinion, this book ought *not* to be a success. If the people who will really like it and understand it are the only ones to buy it, it should sell about 1,000 copies. However, if you wish to take a risk on the name of the author, and the hope that about 5,000 readers may get curious as to the content of his meditations, then you can have the book.

I cannot say that this book fits in with any of the current fashions in spirituality either. In fact, it is nothing but an ordinary book by an ordinary monk.

Thanks indeed for the references you send me on solitude. A large proportion of the saints venerated in the calendar of the Order were hermits. I do not think we have the issue of the *Analecta* which you refer to, but we can get it.

As far as I know, my Superiors must have decided by now what is to become of me, but Dom James has not yet written to me from Cîteaux. As time goes on, I begin to think that it is not going to be easy for me to get a real permission to lead the eremitical life here, still less to leave and go to Frascati. By now I think I can say that I have become more or less indifferent. If God wants me to be a solitary, I will be His kind of solitary, no matter what may be the exterior conditions that may be imposed on me. Of this I am certain, and I am beginning to find that as time goes on I do become, inevitably, more and more of a solitary, and that the very moves which are supposed to destroy my tending to solitude have the effect of making me interiorly—and even exteriorly—more of a hermit. Why, then, should I worry much about what is to be done? I shall probably never reach such a neat and beautiful solution as your good Fr. Bernth, but what of it?

THOMAS MERTON TO JEAN LECLERCQ

December 3, 1955

You had heard from Dom Gabriel Sortais . . . about my vocation. But you had evidently not heard all that eventually came about. It happens that I am now master of novices! In fact, I am somewhat more of a cenobite than I expected to be. Strange things can happen in the mystery of one's vocation.*

As I am master of novices, Father Abbot desires me to devote my full time to the souls of my charges. He will not allow me to consider your kind invitation to

---

*In the summer of 1955 Merton volunteered to be master of novices, replacing Walter Helmstetter, who had been elected Abbot of Gethsemani's fourth foundation, Our Lady of the Genesee, in upstate New York. So, rather than taking up residence in the fire-lookout tower at Gethsemani, Merton wisely offered his services as master of choir novices, a position he held for the next ten years. On August 20, 1965, he became a full-time hermit on the property at Gethsemani.

join you in your project on the Psalms, although I want to express my gratitude to you for asking me. In any event, I feel that I would not be erudite enough to join you, but my job in the novitiate makes it entirely out of the question. I shall cease to be a writer at least as long as I am in charge of the novices. The prospect does not trouble me. I care very little what I do now, so long as it is the will of God.

Will He someday bring me after all to perfect solitude? I do not know. One thing is sure, I have made as much effort in that direction as one can make without going beyond the limits of obedience. My only task now is to remain quiet, abandoned, and in the hands of God. I have found a surprising amount of interior solitude among my novices, and even a certain exterior solitude which I had not expected. This is, after all, the quietest and most secluded corner of the monastery. So I am grateful to God for fulfilling many of my desires when seeming to deny them. I know that I am closer to Him, and that all my struggles this year formed part of His plan. I am at peace in His will. Thank you for your part in the affair. If you see Dom Maurizio, will you also thank him for all his kindness and for the invitation which, alas, I was unable to accept?

I am delighted to hear that Giustiniani has finally appeared. I have not yet received a copy, but I am hoping that some will come soon.

I am very glad that you like the meditations. I do not feel the book is adequate or complete. But since I can do little or nothing to remedy matters now, I will have to leave it as a fragment. I look forward to hearing news of it. I entrust you with the care of getting it approved by Dom Gabriel Sortais.

Please pray for me and for my novices. Your course on "Grammar and Eschatology" sounds interesting; the only thing in the title that I find difficult is the word "grammar." That, precisely, is the hook. If you publish these lectures in a volume, I hope you will not forget to send me one.

Meanwhile, for my part I am happily lecturing on Cassian. What could be better material in my situation? Although I cannot live like Abbot Isaac, Nesteros, or Piamon, I feel that they are my fathers and my friends.

THOMAS MERTON TO JEAN LECLERCQ

February 6, 1956

It is already a long time since I had the pleasure of receiving your finished and published work on Giustiniani—after all this wait. It is a splendid book, and reading it again in French I do not hesitate to say that it is the one of your books which I most enjoy. I think it is really a landmark in spiritual books of our time, even though Giustiniani is not himself a figure of towering importance. Nevertheless, this statement of the perennial value of the eremitical life is an important one, one which needs to be made and one which will have a significant effect. I predict that it will be in fact one of the most influential of your books—perhaps not by the number of the souls it influences, but by their quality and by the depth of their reaction.

My new life as master of novices progresses from day to day. It is an unfamiliar existence to which I often have difficulty in adapting myself. I sometimes feel overcome with sheer horror at having to talk so much and appear before others as an example. I believe that God is testing the quality of my desire for solitude, in which perhaps there was an element of escape from responsibility. But nevertheless the desire remains the same, the conflict is there, but there is nothing I can do but ignore it and press forward to accomplish what is evidently the will of God.

I have abandoned all writing now.

Please ask Our Lord to guide me in the new tract of desert which He has opened before me.

THOMAS MERTON TO JEAN LECLERCQ

Leclercq, of course, found Thoughts in Solitude *suitable for his series, but Merton was vacillating about publishing it (it was called* Thirty-seven Meditations *in an earlier version).*

[An undated fragment, Fall 1956]
. . . More than that, I hope the book is suitable. I was especially happy that the few pages on solitude were left untouched. I thought for sure that the censors of the Order would tear them in little pieces and shower

them over my head like confetti—as one of my Latin masters in England once did with a Latin syntax examination which he did not like.

It is a pleasure to feel that this volume will be printed under your auspices. I am so tired of being a notorious author, and being edited by another monk makes me feel at least somewhat more of a monk myself.

Although I have not had occasion to write to you for some time, I have thought of you often in this year sacred to the memory of Peter the Venerable, and indeed I think he has watched over me, for this summer I had occasion to visit the Benedictines at St. John's, Collegeville—for a summer workshop in psychiatry and pastoral care (useful for novice masters!). There I felt more closely united to all my Benedictine Brothers at La Pierre-qui-Vire, Clervaux, etc. There too I ran across one James Kritzeck, a student at Princeton, who had the proofs of the memorial volume on the great Abbot of Cluny. I glanced at them, but looked in vain for your article on Peter the Venerable and hermits. Perhaps it will be in the final edition. I look forward to reading it.

As time goes on it seems that I grow closer to the state in which nothing at all is written. I have not attempted anything like a book since I became novice master. But with the inveterate itch of the writer I have turned some novitiate conferences into a pamphlet. Of this, too, I shall soon be cured. I have spent the year teaching a course on Cassian, on the Cistercian Consuetudines, and now on St. Bernard—I am just begin-

ning. I am eager to see your lectures given at Sant'
Anselmo, which you said would probably be published.
What I am doing is nothing at all, just an introduction
for novices, and very superficial.

I do hope this winter to be able to set several things
aside and apply myself to the study of Clement and
Origen, and the Alexandrians, and the Fathers of
Egypt, and the sources of monastic spirituality in
general. Is there anything new on this, in the last year
or so? More and more I feel attracted to Evagrius. The
new Sources Chrétiennes re-edition of Didoque de Pho-
tice is to me delightful and nourishing. I have become
very fond of it and am almost inseparable from it. I like
Didoque very much.

The question of solitude is no longer any kind of a
question. I leave everything in the hands of God and
find my solitude in His will, without being theatrical or
glowingly pious about it. I am content. But the right
kind of contentment is a perfect solitude. When one is
more or less content with the "nothing" that is at hand,
one finds in it everything. I do not mean "nothing" in a
·tragic, austere sense, but the plain nothing which is the
something of every day. The life of a Benedictine does
not require all the fierce strippings of a St. John of the
Cross, but the common way without exaltation (even in
nothingness) is enough.

October 19, 1957

It has been a long time since I have had the satisfaction of writing to you. However, Father Abbot has preferred that, since I am master of novices, I should not occupy myself much with matters of business. And this is as it should be, except that it does mean I also have less contact with friends in other monasteries.

In this case it is necessary for me to write to you. For a long time I have heard nothing whatever about the French translation of *Thirty-seven Meditations.* That is not strange, as I have not heard anything about any other business either. Except for rare cases in which my intervention was necessary. Hence I have no idea whether or not the book is being published, or has been published, or will be published. The main reason for my writing is the hope that the book has not yet been published, and the further hope that perhaps something has happened to change your mind about its publication.

In the time that has elapsed since the writing of the book I have been able to see it in a new light. This new light is by no means favorable. I realize that the book has very serious deficiencies, in fact that it is practically worthless. No doubt a publisher may allow himself to be blinded to the real nature of a book by the possibilities for its wide diffusion, due to some accidental circumstance. But I am persuaded that if this book is published, it will be a serious mistake. Of course, I myself am to blame for not having noticed this before. However, I hope that for some reason or other the publication of the French translation has been blocked, and even that you may have decided not to publish the book at all, and have hesitated to tell me so. If that is the case, then I will be very relieved. And I will urge you to return the manuscript to me and we can forget all about it with the greatest of satisfaction. Or even if you still are thinking of publishing the book, but the work of printing has not yet been begun, I would like to urge you to reconsider the whole thing, in the light of what I have just said.

If, on the other hand, the book has been published, I shall be forced to accept the inevitable. Perhaps the book will offer me the consolation of being less bad in French than in English, but I doubt it.

The past year, in which I have been almost exclusively occupied with the novices and with my own spiritual life, has been for me a very pleasant one, and I think with considerable satisfaction that in the future I will probably have no further reason to write anything much, although I suppose I will always be called upon here and there to do some small job for the monastery. I have not seen your book yet. I am trying to get hold of a copy, for I imagine it is very interesting and will be very valuable to us.

November 13, 1957

I was relieved to hear that the book had not yet been published. Father Abbot is willing to allow me to stop publication altogether, but in deference to the translator I am willing to reconsider the matter.

After my decision to throw the book away, I came across the original first version. The version I sent you to be translated is somewhat different, not so much in the material as in the way it is organized. I find that in the original, more spontaneous and less "systematic" arrangement of the chapters, the book regains some life and quality, and is more or less bearable. Even then it is awfully slight and superficial, and has little real religious value. It is nothing but a sort of philosophical notebook without much depth or point. Why should such a thing be imposed on the Catholic reader by monks? It is bad enough to have so much of it coming from the rest of the clergy.

However, rather than just give the Sister a fee and suppress her translation (which would hardly be comforting to anyone) I will reconsider the whole project. But in order to do so I would like to have the manuscript of the translation. Perhaps by rearranging the material in its original order, presenting it somewhat differently, etc., I can make it less bad. At least I hope I will be able to do something to arrange the matter to everyone's satisfaction and not just to save my own face. Please pray that we will end up with whatever decision is best in God's eyes.

I was overwhelmed and edified by Dom Winandy's retirement to solitude.* Clearly, your Order is much more clear-sighted than ours. You have the flexibility which we so sadly, so miserably lack. I am afraid there is a rigidity endemic in the very structure of the Cistercian Order which in the end will stifle all serious development in the right direction. True, it may also prevent development in the wrong direction. At least a negative advantage.

Your work on the History of Spirituality sounds interesting. May I ask what is this project? I shall be very interested in hearing more about it and you can certainly count on our prayers. Meanwhile I shall strive to attain your other book, which will not be difficult. I do not reproach you for not having millions of copies to distribute to everyone in the New World as well as in the Old.

May I ask your prayers in turn for a new hope of mine—that perhaps someday we may make a foundation in the Andes, and that I may be sent there if God wills. Again, if we were only a little more flexible, we could do it tomorrow. However, the Lord is bringing us good postulants from Latin America and I am sure the project will one day mature.

*Dom Jacques Winandy, former Abbot of Clervaux, Leclercq's monastery in Luxembourg, went to live as a hermit on the island of Martinique.

May 22, 1958

Some time ago questions were asked about the French translation of *Thoughts in Solitude* (*Les Chemins de la joie*). You remember that you had this translated by a Benedictine nun and it was to have been published by Les Editions d'Histoire et d'Art. I remember that I myself complicated matters somewhat when I hesitated about the publication of this book in English or in French. The French ms. was sent to me and I returned it eventually with the consent to its publication.

Nothing more has ever been heard of it. Recently there was question of offering to some other publisher the French rights for this book. I heard this from my agent, and told them to hold off until we could find out something definite about your translation. Will you please let me know where matters stand? If your publisher does not want this translation you have, perhaps it could go to some other publisher. Let me know please.

Most of the trouble comes from the fact that I have been out of contact with you for so long. It is a pleasure to greet you again, and to ask your prayers. I heard Dom Jacques Winandy is in Martinique. I hope he will pray for me too. I naturally keep a certain desire for solitude in my heart and cannot help but hope that someday it may be realized. But I no longer have any thought or desire of transferring to another Order. I believe that to move from one institution to another is simply futile. I do not believe that there is any institutional solution for me. I can hope, however, that perhaps I might gain permission to live alone, in the shadow of this monastery, if my Superiors will ever permit it. I do not think that there is any other fully satisfactory way for me to face this, but to seek to live my own life with God. I am not pushing this, however, simply praying, hoping, and waiting. I hope you will pray for me also.

JEAN LECLERCQ TO THOMAS MERTON

Vichy, Allier

June 2, 1959

I never heard, myself, about your ms. since the last time you asked to have it again in order to modify it according to the censors or to your own evolution. I realize now that you sent it back to Wittmann, but I fancy Wittmann's business is not prosperous and that he is not willing to publish the text. Do write to him, directly or through the agent (if you prefer so and let me know, I'll write myself). And please do not forget the nun who translated it.

I am very glad to hear that you remain yourself. The police of the ideas [thought police] will never prevail against a real vocation. The trouble is that too much publicity has been given to your case (apart from your books, by the inquiries you sent to many people). Now, with more silence, you will probably come to a peaceful solution. Yes, Dom Winandy is in Martinique, full of spiritual joy. He has been a hermit in Switzerland and hopes to be a hermit again in Martinique. But being an Abbot, as you are an author, his case is not merely a private one, and men in charge of the police of the ideas feel obliged to take many cautions. But, here again, with time and silence, life and grace will prevail.

When you say changing Orders is "futile," I suppose you speak *for you*, and for you it is perhaps true. But there have always been transfers in monasticism; it is still admitted in the Church that a religious may change Orders. Many Trappist monasteries have monks who have been in other Orders before, and you remember that St. Bernard wrote many men to change Orders. If a vocation is impossible in one Order, the solution is to change robes. It is only when we "absolutize" an institution that we admit that it must prevail against the spirit, against the spirit of liberty of which St. Bernard spoke so often . . .

THOMAS MERTON TO JEAN LECLERCQ

October 8, 1959

The hope of finding a more solitary life now seems to be quite well founded. There are very definite possibilities, but also there are still very great obstacles to be overcome, not the least of which is my own Abbot. But this time I have an entirely different attitude. I have very many solid reasons for thinking that solitude, for me, is truly God's will, and this gives me a more calm and confident outlook. There is no need to press the point unduly for my own interests, because more than my own interests are at stake. It is God's cause, not mine. Furthermore, I am very much aware that it is not merely a matter of "natural attraction," because if I "followed nature" (as the consecrated and sacrosanct phrase has it) I would certainly stay here, where I am in comfort and where everything is well established and where I can live a respected and humanly productive existence as a well-known writer.

It does not seem that a solitary life here is any solution, or that it would be possible in any real sense. But I have hopes of a solution which, if it works, I know will be very effective. I rely very much on your prayers and on those of others with similar interests. Pray too that my health may hold up. At the moment it seems to be slightly threatened, but I believe it is just a case of one of those disturbances of the system which come along when a great change has to be made, and which in a sense slow one down for the corner.

I am glad of this opportunity to ask your good prayers, and those of all others who feel inclined to help me in this one thing which really seems to me important, and beside which everything else I do is as nothing. I certainly attach not the slightest importance to any writing, and I know now that I no longer "need" to write as I did when writing was a necessary outlet in the cenobitic life. But no one knows how he will look at such a thing under different conditions. I am not preoccupied with the question at all.

Has Frascati planned and made a Camaldolese foundation in the U.S.? I hear rumors to that effect. That is not what attracts me at the moment, though. I think I have something better. I hope so, in the Lord.

Clervaux

October 23, 1959

Yes, Dom Maurizio of Frascati is now in the U.S. Their General Chapter has decided to make a foundation there. It is now on the property which the Bishop of Steubenville put at their disposal (Holy Family Hermitage, Camaldolese, McConnelsville, Ohio).

I perfectly understand your own vocation. I do not think it is an illusion. In the black monachism, the idea of the legitimacy of the solitary life is making slow but solid progress, I think. I hope and pray that you may not only find but follow your own way. Our own new Abbot, after he has seen our new hermit in Switzerland, realized that it was serious. Dom Winandy is perfectly happy in his solitude over the seas.

Let's pray for one another!

Merton finds himself caught between his desire to help Leclercq with the French translation of Thoughts in Solitude *and his commitments to his existing French agent and publishers. He decides to leave the whole matter in Leclercq's hands. It was published as* Les Chemins de la joie *in 1961.*

November 19, 1959

There you are. I do not know if it is as simple as all that. I am not a "business man," fortunately.

Now I shall tell you, in confidence, something more interesting and more monastic. I have asked the Congregation of Religious for an exclaustration so as to go to Mexico and become a hermit near the Benedictine monastery of Cuernavaca. Dom Gregorio [Lemercier] will take me on and encourages me very much. This is really what I have been looking for a long time. I have good hopes of succeeding with the Congregation, but the Superiors are dead set against this move. Dom James is at present in Rome, where the Most Rev. Father has summoned him.* But though knowing that this must have something to do with my case, I do not know exactly what may happen. There must be some other matter there, because I do not believe that they have made Fr. Abbot come to Rome merely in order to block my indult [permission from Rome to leave]. At present there are some questions which have arisen respecting another monk from here, who has the same problem as I, but with certain canonical complications which are perhaps the fault of the Superiors. It may be

*Dom James Fox was called to Rome at this time mainly because of Merton's request for an exclaustration. As was expected, the request was refused.

for that . . . But in spite of that, I still have the hope that at the same time they will let me go to make the experiment. I am very happy and I think I shall succeed well with the grace of God. Truly, I am who I am and I always have the writer's temperament, but I am not going down there to write, nor to make myself known, but on the contrary to disappear, to find solitude, obscurity, poverty. To withdraw *above all* from the collective falsity and injustice of the U.S., which implicate so much the Church in this country and our monastery.

I tell you this (and I beg of you not to talk about it) in order to ask your prayers, and also, if you should happen to be in Rome these days, to take my side somewhat with Dom Gabriel [Sortais], who respects you very much. (To him, yes, you may speak of this.) I even reckon a little on the Procurator of the Benedictines—but this is up to Dom Gaspris, I think. In a word, if you can do anything for me, I beg of you in your charity to do so.

In any case, if the matter turns out well this time, I continue. I do not think this is the time to let go, whatever it may be. My Benedictine vocation is, I am sure, a solitary vocation, at least relatively, and primitive. It may be that my health cannot withstand the intestinal illnesses in the tropics; in that case I shall recommence the attempt elsewhere, perhaps in Europe or in the regions of the U.S. where there are Indians. If you write a word to me on these matters, I beg of you to address it to me *sub secreto*—conscience matter.

Clervaux

November 28, 1959

I pray a lot for you. All that you tell me interests me intensely. It is always difficult to see clearly into ourselves, around us. It is then that one appreciates the benefit of obedience to an authority, which, abundantly informed about all the aspects of a problem, sufficiently distant and elevated to be impartial, can judge about us better than we ourselves. I am, however, an old Roman; for twenty-six years I have been living partly in Rome. Association with history has made me see the limits of all institutions in which human beings intervene, including the Roman Church (and the others). But I must also say, because I know it, and have evidences of it, that serious matters are seriously examined in Rome, and that all guarantees are taken so that the decisions may be objective and not influenced by this or that party. They remain for us the surest indications of the will of God. I pray that the one you are expecting will and that you will accept it, whatever it may be, with joy.

THOMAS MERTON TO JEAN LECLERCQ

December 24, 1960

I learned late in the fall that you had been in America this summer. What a pity that you did not come down to Gethsemani; I would have enjoyed seeing you and talking to you. I am sure you were able to accomplish a lot of good at St. John's. I intend to read your article on "La Spiritualité Vanniste," as I think I will write a study on Dom Calmet for the *American Benedictine Review*. I wonder if you can suggest any interesting materials? I am basing myself so far on the contemporary biography of Dom Calmet in French, on his commentary on the Rule, and such references as are made in the ordinary histories of the O.S.B.

My personal problems seem to be working themselves out in a way. A very fine little hermitage has been built in a nice site; it is for the purpose of dialogue and conversations with Protestant ministers and professors, but it also serves for solitude and I have at least a limited permission to use it part-time. This is to a great extent a hopeful solution and I find that if I can have at least *some* real solitude and silence it makes a tremendous difference. It can at least help to stave off the kind of crisis that arose in 1959 when I felt it was necessary to change my situation and go elsewhere. As long as this solution exists, this can be avoided. I am in any case getting more and more indifferent. I know that God Himself is above and beyond the solutions and decisions of men, and that if my desires come from Him, He Himself will not have any trouble in leading me where He wants me, and giving me the solitude He desires. At least I know that my interior solitude grows more and more.

Best wishes and prayers for the New Year. Remember me please in your prayers and Masses, sometimes. I hope if you come to this country again we may meet one another here.

Via di Torre Rossa, Rome
December 31, 1960

If I did not meet you, I at least met Dom James at Genesee [Cistercian monastery near Rochester, New York]. I shall be in the States again next May and June, conducting retreats at St. John's [Collegeville, Minnesota] and Regina Laudis [Benedictine abbey in Connecticut] and giving talks elsewhere as much as the schedule allows. I enjoyed immensely my discovery of monasticism in your country, under all its different forms. But of course, I only go where I am invited; I never take the initiative.

I am glad to know that your personal problems are solved. I think you (they) finally came across the traditional solution: some solitude, for those who need it, and it ought to be found within the institution itself. You call for a Western Athos: but that was traditionally realized in medieval monasteries, when the institutions were flexible enough to give different sorts of souls different ways of living the same monastic life.

I am sending you by surface mail an offprint of my "Spiritualité Vanniste." I do not know anything about Dom Calmet. I think it would be necessary to read his works.

I am giving lectures this year at Sant'Anselmo on the traditional vocabulary and concepts of contemplative life, which I hope to publish soon. The matter interests me, and a small group of monks of different colors attends.

Yes, I will pray for you.

[P.S.] I have just sent to the printers a paper on monastic priesthood according to monastic tradition. Dom Laurence enjoyed it.* May it be helpful!

JEAN LECLERCQ TO THOMAS MERTON

Clervaux

April 4, 1961

Thank you for your news. I am glad that the book will soon appear. I think that it may contribute—and I just realize that the holding up of the French text has been providential—to the problem which is one of the many that the Holy See has now to face in prevision of the [Vatican] Council. As far as I have any information, I have a good impression. We have begun to move: God will do the rest. [Vatican Council announced.] I have just finished a short paper on the matter, in collaboration with Dom [Pierre] Doyère (cf. *Dictionnaire de spiritualité*, fasc. 28, 982), which his Abbot and mine have approved.

---

*Dom Laurence Bourget, a monk of Spencer, at this time was the American Definitor at the Generalate in Rome, where Leclercq would frequently visit when in Rome.

I am glad that *Love of Learning* may prove useful (it's nice and amusing that neither in French nor in English anyone, not even you, ever quotes the title exactly); everybody thinks of "loving God" [*The Love of Learning and the Desire for God*]. Already some American scholars are lamenting the fact that it has been produced by Fordham as a "devotional book": they think that it is also for scholars. The reviewer in *Speculum* (Medieval Academy of America) emphasizes this. The aim is to reconcile these sorts of separated Brothers, separated sometimes even inside monastic life. I also wrote an article in English which will soon be forthcoming on monastic priesthood which has been approved by people of both sides because my solution (the traditional one) is a middle one. This may help also. In this field, again, I now know that we may expect something from the Holy See. And for the Brothers' problem as well.

I am not particularly against journals, not even among monks, and I do not remember ever having expressed publicly a disagreement with you on this point. I know of many people (mainly Scandinavians, Anglo-Saxons) who have been very edified by *The Sign of Jonas*.

One of our monks enjoys *Contacts* and your article on Athos. He is not a Superior at all, but just a starets, and the spiritual father of many of us.

In my schedule I still have a full week, from June 20 to 27, between a retreat at Collegeville and a talk at the Benedictine Institute of Sacred Theology at St. Joseph,

Minnesota. No invitation came from Gethsemani: I fully understand . . .

> Abbey of New Melleray
> Dubuque, Iowa
> June 11, 1961

I am sending back to you one of the Karl Rahner volumes, *Free Speech in the Church*. I enjoyed it very much. One of the two monks I was with one afternoon sent it to me. But I cannot remember his name. But you will know.

The visit to New Melleray is very beneficial for me. This young community is very responsive to my little monastic message.

I have great memories of you all at Gethsemani. Please convey my gratitude to Dom James.

> Clervaux
> July 12, 1961

I sought the Imprimatur to *Living in Silence*. What I found was the one concerning *The Last of the Fathers*. But I am sure now that I sent the Imprimatur to the publisher.

I have seen at Minneapolis a copy of *Alone with God*. I guess you have received it by now.

Thank you again to your Reverend Father and all of you for your kindness and hospitality. Stays at New Melleray [Iowa] and Berryville [Virginia] have been extremely beneficial for me. I come back with still more admiration than last year for your country and its monasticism.

THOMAS MERTON TO JEAN LECLERCQ

June 10, 1963

How are you? I do not know where this letter will find you, but I suppose the best thing to do at this season is to send it to Clervaux, and it can follow you.

What I want to ask is: can I borrow an offprint of your article on the "*Reclus et recluses dans le diocèse de Metz*" from the *Rev. Hist. Ecclés. du Diocèse de Metz*? I hate to trouble you about this. I hope it is possible for you to lend it to me without too much inconvenience, or to tell me where I might perhaps be able to get a photocopy of the article, or a film or something. I want to do a little study of Grimlaicus,* perhaps for the *Collectanea* [*Cisterciensia*] or perhaps for the new *Monastic Studies* of Berryville, which is very well done.

The thing that interests me about Grimlaicus is not the rather impractical setup he has devised for recluses,

---

*Grimlaicus (or Grimlaic) was a ninth-century priest/scholar from the diocese of Metz who wrote a Rule, or spiritual guide, for solitaries. The article was wrongly attributed to Jean Leclercq (it was written by Canon Jacques Leclercq). The study Merton speaks of doing never materialized.

but the spirit that animates his Rule. It is as far as I can see the closest Western counterpart to the oriental idea of the megaloschemos* in the common life. This has a great deal of importance just at the present moment, when I think we need to understand the need to allow *growth* and *development* in mature monks toward a more deeply contemplative life. At the present, as you know, there is an exaggerated fear that all attempts to develop present some kind of temptation or danger, and also there is fear that if one legitimate aspiration is encouraged, a lot of less legitimate ones will arise to bother the Superior.

Things are developing well here, however. I received permission to take some time in solitude up at the hermitage, and so far I have had six full days up there, with more to come. Not allowed to sleep there, or say Mass there, but what I have had so far is a great godsend. It has certainly settled any doubts I may have had about the need for real solitude in my own life. Though I realize that I am not the ideal of an absolute hermit, since my solitude is partly that of an intellectual and poet, still it is a very real inclination for solitude, and when I have continuous solitude for a more or less extended period, it means a great deal and is certainly the best remedy for the tensions and pressures that I generate when I am with the community. It is indeed the only really satisfactory remedy that I have been able to find.

*A monk of the highest rank in Orthodox Monasticism who wore the "great habit."

Distractions and "recreations" with visitors and active retreat work, etc. do absolutely nothing to help. Also, this little bit of solitude helps me to appreciate the real values that do exist in the common life, though they certainly manage to get hidden when I get too much of them. I hope to take more time in retreat later in the summer or in the early fall. And perhaps get a day at a time more frequently.

There has been a lot of talk about our Monastic Formation course, but actually it does not amount to much. However, please let us know if you are in this country, because I am very anxious to have you give the group a talk if possible, or two or three even. But if you can spare us even a small amount of time I would be delighted, and we would all be indebted to you. So if you are in the Midwest, I hope you can give us a little time and I would be glad to see you again.

Any suggestions you may have about Grimlaicus will be very welcome, and I do hope I can get a look at your article. I liked very much some of your pages on St. Gregory in the *Histoire de la spiritualité chrétienne*. I have used your material there in a long article I have done on the question of "The Humanity of Christ in Prayer" as it was seen by the monastic Fathers. For them it was no "problem" as it seems to have been in the time of St. Teresa [of Avila].

Clervaux

June 18, 1963

Glad to read you! I am well and, strangely enough, in Clervaux.

My trip in the States last autumn ended at New Melleray, where I had to fly from Boston, having lectured at Harvard. I spent two days discussing the building plan and then went straight to Rome. It was an exciting Council winter, though I did not go out much. But the Council was everywhere. What a wonderful Church experience. Then I conducted a retreat at St.-Benoit-sur-Loire, and then went back to Italy again for a retreat to the Knights of Malta and the Noblesse Catholique Internationale, where, funnily enough, I came across Ned O'Gorman. After that I spent five weeks in Toumliline, Morocco. For Easter I was in Clervaux. I shall not be going to the States this year: I am engaged for a tour of the Trappist abbeys in Ireland and Caldey [Wales] again, after lecturing at the Athos Congress in Venice on September 4. Next year I am booked for Central Africa, where there are great needs and great hopes. I have discovered Islam and am planning to organize a symposium at Toumliline at the request of the Prior on "Monasticism in Christianity, in Islam, and Their Relations." I wrote a short paper in *Images de Toumliline*. Do you get this review? If not, I could send you a copy when I have one to spare. Do you know of any scholars (no matter what denomination) who would be interested in this problem and whom I could invite? [Gustav] von Guinebaum of the University of California seems to be all right, but there must be others too.

The article on Grimlaic is by Canon J. [Jacques] Leclercq, written by mistake in [*Dictionnaire de*] *Spiritualité* (this will be corrected in the English edition). But I have the offprint and have mailed it to you. I think your idea on the megaloschema is good. We must find some way to favor progress without creating disorder. The danger in the Latin Church is always—at least in our times—to set up new juridical categories, fixed forever.

Have you seen the monastic chronicle in *Irenikon* 63, 1? The article I wrote on the priesthood in the same issue brings in many reactions, most of which are favorable.

I have just been reading some good pages by René Roques, *Structures théologiques*, Paris, Presses Universitaires de France, 1963, on the theology of the monastic life according to Denys: it is a good attempt to situate monasticism in the sacramental order within the priesthood.

I am glad of the good news you give about yourself. Your experience is a good one. You are not a unique case.

Yes, *Monastic Studies* is very nicely produced.

I had a good chat here recently with Ed Rice.

July 23, 1963

It was very kind of you to send the material on Grim-laic. I will keep working on the idea of an article about him and these two pieces will be of great use, even though they are by another Leclerc without the "q." I can never figure out whether there are two or *three* Leclerc(q)'s. Usually you are working in different fields and do not get in each other's way. There is, funnily enough, another Thomas Merton, in England, a "Sir" Thomas, no less, at Oxford and a collector of paint-ings. He is rather older and more venerable than I so he must be irritated if people think he has become a monk and written his autobiography. I have never run across him.

Ed Rice sent me your essay on the Rule and *pre-senza nelmondo* [presence in the world], which is excel-lent, and I am at present translating it for *Jubilee*. I think it will, or should, have a great deal of meaning in this country. I do not think that the American monas-teries, even of our Order, have got out of this national obsession with productivity. It is one of the great delu-sions and temptations of the age, especially here, and it is certainly the one thing that wrecks monastic voca-tions, much more than the love of the pleasures of the world. Are they after all such great pleasures? We are more tempted by ambition.

Father Abbot has been away visiting foundations. His letters always give a desolating impression of cattle ranches, alfalfa crops, prunes, hay, beef cattle, diesel tractors and other elaborate machinery. And really, a few slogans about the absolute superiority of the "contemplative life" added on at the end do little to relieve this sense of desolation: a spiritual desert worse than anything else.

I envy you going to Africa. I think it is a very important place now. Toumliline [Morocco] is a place I admire greatly. Dom Denis Martin met and spoke to me briefly here. Naturally, I did not have permission to visit with him: he is one of those "dangerous" Benedictines who are experimenting with a new kind of monastic life. I have written to him but I suppose he must be on the black list for mail, too. Perhaps someday I may travel somewhere, and if I do I hope to go to Toumliline. Please give him my best regards if you write to him or see him. Do please send me a copy of *Images de Toumliline*. It probably comes to the monastery, but nobody sees it if it does. I am not receiving the bulletins from La Vierge des Pauvres either, though they did begin to come. In a word, Benedictines are dangerous here, Father! Dom Aelred Graham invited me, very kindly, to spend a little time at Portsmouth for a vacation. I was tempted to reply that it would be easier for me to get permission to take a mistress than it would be to visit a Benedictine monastery, even one that was not primitive.

In any case I hope your visits to the monasteries, etc. in Africa will be very fruitful for you and for them. If the Church would really reach all the Negroes, what life there would be! I send you a little piece I have written about the Negro situation in America. Again I am perhaps a little beyond the limits of what a monk is theoretically supposed to do, and yet I am convinced that today at least one or two monks should speak of these things, especially in America. What do you think?

[P.S.] I have been talking to the novices about St. Pachomius and reading some of the material translated from Coptic. He has been too little known: there is much in him that is of great interest.

JEAN LECLERCQ TO THOMAS MERTON

Mount Melleray Abbey
County Waterford, Ireland
October 26, 1963

I have just visited all the Trappist abbeys of Ireland, and visited again those of England. Everywhere I could see the seeds of a future new monastic culture, new combination of Trappist fervor with a certain knowledge and intelligence. I am very comforted. God not only sent vocations, but helps them to develop. Everywhere I found boys who got their vocations through you. I even promised to Brothers Brendan and Francis of Nunraw Abbey, Haddington [Scotland], England, to get from you an autograph. They love this text and image. Enclosing a photo and text for you to write a word and your name, and send it to them or to me for them? Thanks.

I am on my way to Via di Torre Rossa, Rome.

The Council develops very well, I think. Finally!

November 10, 1963

First of all I hope the translation of your article on Benedictine work reached you in Ireland. It was sent on to you by the editors of *Monastic Studies*, from Berryville. I am afraid *Jubilee* did not take the article after all, feeling it was "too technical." But *Monastic Studies* will publish it.

Then, thanks for your two offprints. I was very touched by many of the beautiful references to your piece on *sedere* [to sit]. Did you know that the fourteenth-century English mystic Rolle was known as "the sitier" [the sitter]? He has some nice things about sitting as the most favorable position for contemplation. Of course, the Buddhists of the Far East have many texts on this too. A Zen artist, Sengai, did a picture of a turnip with this short poem: "Turnips and Zen monks / are best when they sit well."

The one on the early history of eremitism in the West is excellent, and again it has many fine examples, as well as showing that one must not take a stereotyped view of the solitary life. For some people, the solitary life is their only way of truth, and it is *their* truth precisely insofar as it is not imposed on them from the outside. Some people are congenitally incapable of understanding this. It is a perpetual scandal, especially to the standard Cistercian mentality. On the other hand, people like Dom Augustine Baker and Dame Gertrude More [English Benedictines] have a wonderful sense of all this. I hope to do a study on Gertrude More for Stanbrook [English Benedictine convent]. There is also a piece of mine on her and Baker in the *Collectanea* [*Cisterciensia*], coming up soon, I believe.

By the way, I was very amused on Cistercians and hermits, in *Studia Monastica*, after the two Vitae of Boniface's disciples, which were charming.

There are many things to thank you for.

JEAN LECLERCQ TO THOMAS MERTON

Clervaux
November 12, 1963

Thanks for the translation on Benedictine work, which I received in due time. I realize it was not for *Jubilee*. They surprised me by giving a photo of me with a short notice in which they mentioned the problem of monastic simplicity. I asked them to send me one or two copies of this October issue. I hope they will.

I had some other, better texts and oriental pictures on *sedere*. But in the paper I wanted to restrict myself to the Middle Ages. Thanks for letting me know some others.

I shall be glad to see your papers on Gertrude More and on Baker. I think this fear of solitude is recent, typically nineteenth-century.

The author of the *Admonitio ad filium spiritualem* is St. Basil. This has been established by Paul Lehmann in a study in the Sitzungsberichte of Munich, with a provisional critical edition. My collaborator, Dom [Henri] Rochais, Momont, Juignac Demontmoreau, Charente, France, has an offprint. You could write and ask him to lend it to you.

I am sending you my last copy of Hausherr in the Tholles presentation.

I began my teaching in the form of colloqui on "New Monastic Problems and Tendencies": thirty people, half of whom, at least, are Trappists (Fr. Chrysogonus [Waddell], or Callistus [Peterson]). The last time I invited Fr. Bede Griffiths of India to tell us about his effort to set up a Christian ashram, and the colloquium was good. That opens up many minds who never dreamed that things could be "not-as-in-Bellefontaine."

Thanks for the Nunraw boys. They will be so happy.

[P.S.] There is a large manuscript diffusion of the *Admonitio* in Western medieval monasticism, where this text had wide influence. I mentioned this in my Venice talk on the relations between Eastern and Western monasticism, for the millenary of Athos. As soon as I have this offprint I will send it to you. As I think your translation should be based on or checked by Lehmann's critical text, I think the best for you would be to order this booklet: P. Lehmann, *Die Admonitio Basilii ad filium spiritualem*, in Sitzungsberichte der Bayerischen Akademie, Philosophisch-Historische Klasse, Jahrgang 1955, Wilhelmstrasse 9, Munich 23. 64 pages.

THOMAS MERTON TO JEAN LECLERCQ

January 12, 1964

The other day I sent you a mimeograph of some correspondence that passed between me and Fr. Ronald Roloff, the black sheep of the Benedictine controversy in America. I don't think the correspondence is interesting or satisfactory beyond a certain point, but it may perhaps contribute something restrained and ambiguous to the "Benedictine problem" in America. I have not read Fr. Wilfrid Tunik's book but it looks good.

Dom James is off to the election of the new General of our Order. There is still much speculation of course. We wonder what we will get this time. It would be too much to expect someone like Dom André Louf, so fast. I have facetiously proposed *you* as my choice?! I don't know if you would accept the job, and so I will not press the point. If you refuse, I will campaign for Patriarch Maximos. But I suppose he will refuse also. Hence I will have to accept the one elected by the General Chapter and hope for the best. We have all warned our Abbot that he might get in as the result of a deadlock between the French and Belgian Abbots in the Chapter, and now he is worried about it. Actually, if Dom James were elected it would be a victory for the conservatives and integrists and I am not too anxious for that to happen. How is Dom Willibrord of Tilburg?

I hope our students in Rome are doing well. We hear good news from them quite often. You are a great help and inspiration to them all, and thank God for it!

[P.S.] I am sending you my new book of poems [*Emblems of a Season of Fury*], which are angry and obscure.

JEAN LECLERCQ TO THOMAS MERTON

The following letter refers to an exchange between Merton and Fr. Ronald Roloff, formerly a monk of St. John's Abbey, Collegeville. They began amicably enough, but gradually Roloff's letters expressed strong opposition to Merton and his emphasis on the contemplative dimension of life for monks, both Benedictines and Cistercians. Merton finally gave up and did not mail his last letter to Roloff, although it is preserved in the volume of Merton's letters titled The School of Charity.

Clervaux

March 23, 1964

Sorry I have not yet acknowledged your last papers. I have been talking in different places, and last week at Orval. I had your papers read by various people.

Concerning your correspondence with Fr. Ronald, all that I have to say is this:

1. I am glad to know what Fr. Ronald really thinks, pretty different from what he wrote.
2. The first two pages of his last article in *American Benedictine Review* were full of irony and of the easiest sort. Irony and caricature never help truth and charity.
3. He always emphasized the fact that it is possible to sanctify oneself outside the contemplative life. Granted, of course. The monastic problem is not to know whether this is possible, nor to know whether it is possible to become more holy as a Jesuit than as a monk: it's obvious. The problem is to know whether one has received the vocation, the charism, to go to God in this particular way of life. I had to write a report on this point for the Conciliar Commission. I'll try to send it to you.

Look at the enclosed review (and keep it if you want). I just answered the man that I wanted to call his attention to the fact that Jesus began his ministry by going into the desert.

THOMAS MERTON TO JEAN LECLERCQ

Holy Saturday, 1964

Thanks for your note about Fr. Ronald Roloff. As a matter of fact, I think you have guessed that what he was saying in his letters to me was not his real mind after all. In a couple of recent letters, very long and outspoken, he shows himself to be in reality an activist who has no real taste for the monastic life in its renunciation of the world and in its orientation toward solitude. He seems to be completely convinced that the only genuine monasticism today is one which is busy with education and converting souls, while at the same time he seems deeply confused and troubled about the most genuine and normal monastic works, especially prayer in its more characteristically monastic forms. He is in a word a parish priest or a "Jesuit."

Where he came out most outspokenly was in an attack on an article I had written and sent him. I don't know if you saw it: it is called "The Monk in the Diaspora." A shorter version of it was in *Commonweal*. I sent him the longer mimeographed piece and he found it quite shocking. He accused me of pessimism, defeatism, evasion, etc., etc. All the usual accusations. He ended by giving me a sincere fraternal exhortation to renounce the pernicious influence of [Karl] Rahner and to turn to the saving optimism of Teilhard de Chardin. This I found curious. The division did not seem to me to be self-evident. But apparently that is the attitude some are taking now. One is evaluated in relation to Teilhard, and by this standard monasticism is asked to abandon solitude and prayer to become more open to the world. But the division is made in a very naive fashion. My contention is that there may certainly be an exceptional apostolate for the monks, but that if it exists at all it must be charismatic. And in order to preserve this charismatic quality, the monk must first of all be entirely faithful to the charism of his vocation to solitude and the desert. Otherwise the "apostolate" he attempts to carry out will be an infidelity and a mockery, and in the end he will be neither a good monk nor a good apostle. This seems to be altogether outside his range of thinking. Or at least it is now. I think what happened was that his brethren have read the letters that were mimeographed and had accused him of becoming weak and giving in to the arguments of contemplatives.

I have read with great pleasure the wonderful article of P[atricia] McNulty and her collaborator on the Orientale Lumen in the commemorative Athos volume. It is really magnificent and it will help me a little in my work on recluses. I am keeping on patiently and quietly in this, and will, I hope, eventually begin to get something on paper about Grimlaicus. I also enjoyed the magnificent quote on the Athos hermits, by a fifteenth-century Italian traveler, quoted in the article on the Amalfitan community of Athos. As I told you, I had previously read your own two articles with great pleasure.

Here are a couple of pieces that may interest you, including "The Monk in the Diaspora." Incidentally, I wrote a long answer to Fr. Ronald but then decided not to send it.* If you are interested in seeing a copy of it, I can send it to you. I do not want to waste time arguing where there is no real communication.

*These letters of Thomas Merton to Ronald Roloff were published in *The School of Charity* by Farrar, Straus and Giroux in 1990, which includes the letter about which he writes to Leclercq but which he did not mail to Roloff.

Clervaux

April 15, 1964

I had read and appreciated your "Monk in the Diaspora" before going to a Congress in Italy on Islam and the West in the Middle Ages (where everything happened almost as if Islam had *not* been a religion: military, economic, political, literary, and artistic problems). I shall read it again. I think you are right in maintaining *a certain Christian* pessimism which is also realism. I have noticed a certain danger of *naïve optimisme* in simplifying Teilhard even among monks of your Order. I think there will be an exciting struggle in the years to come on these topics. A certain manner of loving "worldly realities" may lead us to give up all renunciation of the world, flight to God, asceticism, etc. Everything is O.K. in the world which is always making progress, etc. But what about sin, concupiscence, humiliation, all of which are "worldly realities" and facts. And to these answer compunction, penance, humility, etc. I am perhaps too old to understand well these new things, and I hope that I am not at all conservative, but I do think that there are some dangers. You will help us to see clearly. I think Bouyer's pessimism was (except for one or two exaggerated formulas) a Christian realism.

Good news from Monte Cistello: "Our new Abbot General has won the hearts of the new generation by several clear signs of openness and willingness to listen to us and even sympathize with us."

I sent back yesterday the proofs of the article on "Problems and Orientations of Monasticism Today," which will come out in German and in French in the next issue of *Etudes*, a Jesuit review which is read everywhere. Perhaps monastic authority will be obliged to realize that there are problems when the general public talks about them. In the first paragraph, I discussed *your* case, with the sympathy you can imagine. That will not be in *Etudes* because the article was too long, but I hope to publish it in *Revue d'Ascétique et de Mystique*. But I think that all the problems are mentioned; I quoted approved texts and my Abbot was satisfied.

Thanks also for your letter on Fr. Ronald. You are right in not arguing. Ideas go on. What I say (quote) in *Etudes* on U.S. Benedictine life will excite him if he sees it. All the other witnesses quoted were really "monastic," as you will see, though they are Benedictine. What struck me when reading the proofs was that all this vitality which is appearing in new foundations everywhere is extra-Cistercian. So far your Order has given no new fruit. Will it remain barren?

Good news from Dom Winandy in Texas. A man of God: he goes his way, sure of himself and God. A new project of an inter-racial foundation in the Southern states, very good. Dom Winandy knows about the project. New news about Fr. Bede of New Melleray?

Thanks for *Examinatio* in *Collectanea* [*Cisterciensia*].

On May 1 I leave for Dahomey, Togo, and other

African states, giving retreats or conferences in monasteries. At Bouaké, I shall attend the meeting of representatives of forty African monasteries. There will be seven of your Order, but will they be African, or just French-styled, uniformed Trappists? Pray for that.

THOMAS MERTON TO JEAN LECLERCQ

August 2, 1964

I am glad things are moving along with "Diaspora" and especially glad that it has a little meaning for the work of renewal. I am seeing more and more how necessary it is. Unless we have a real reorientation a lot of our younger vocations are going to end in despair and we will not get any new ones. The handwriting is on the wall here: the mere desire to get the monastic life well organized, and the effort to centralize everything in the monastery by reducing the Brothers to complete conformity with the choir (under the pretext of giving them something, when one is taking away their real vocation and the relative flexibility and liberty which it allows them), is an illusion, and when the monks who have ingenuously given their heart to this idea find out that they have been "had" there will be considerable trouble. What we need most of all is the ability to grow and make some creative adaptation to situations that *cannot be defined in advance.* The great danger now seems to be that people are making rigid provisions in the light of situations that have always existed and may not continue to exist much longer.

One thing that has happened here, the kind of absurdity that one might foresee, and quite out of touch with reality. One of the Fathers and several Brothers have worked out a whole elaborate new system of signs, as complex as anything since Ulric of Cluny [Benedictine abbey in France], and even going so far as to include signs that in a rudimentary way attempt to conjugate verbs!!! That is to say, signs indicating endings that modify ideas according to past, future, etc. The next thing will be subjunctives, imperatives, pluperfects, and God knows what else. The author of this genial scheme is going to Rome to study this year; perhaps you will enlighten him. He is determined that this will go through and be accepted for the entire Order, even though one assures him that the very existence of sign language is now brought into question.

I will not continue with this gossip.

Père Placide of Morocco stopped by here in a hurry on a day when I was in the woods, and he did not have time to wait until I might come in, so I did not see him. Fr. Prior had a good talk with him. Have you an offprint of your talk or article that refers to Moslem "monasticism"? This is important for me, as I am doing *chroniques* for the *Collectanea* [*Cisterciensia*] in this field. I will write a résumé.

Thanks for everything.

On August 23, 1964, Leclercq wrote to Merton saying he had heard from the Abbot General, Ignace Gillet, suggesting that the controversial article "The Monk in the Diaspora," which was scheduled to be

published in the Order's journal, Collectanea Cister-
ciensia, *in French, be published in some other journal.
It appeared in Merton's collection of essays* Seeds of
Destruction, *published in 1964 by Farrar, Straus.*

THOMAS MERTON TO JEAN LECLERCQ

August 28, 1964
I am very sorry you have had to have so much trouble
with this "Monk in the Diaspora" article. Dom Ignace
was more opposed to it than I had expected, but I suppose I should have realized that he would have felt in-
sulted.

The best thing seemed to me to simply make a few
simple corrections and emendations in the part of the
text which we both have. I am doing this and sending it
to you. You can make the changes in any way you
wish, with all freedom. As to the part which you have
and I do not, that is to say the very beginning and the
last few pages about the Russians, I leave you to make
any emendation corresponding to the kind of changes I
have made. In particular, I recognize that I was not too
clear about the "diaspora," which tends to be ambiguous because it is in a stage of "becoming," but it seems
to me that it certainly exists in Africa, Asia, etc. But
anyway, that probably needs softening. I note that
the General did not like the camels of Périgueux, but
I will leave them anyway. I think they have their mes-

sage. They come with invisible Magi from the diaspora.

Dom Ignace also mentioned a possible prefatory note by you which would explain that Anglo-Saxon writers (I am really more a Celt than an Anglo-Saxon) are given to irony even when they are serious. I don't know if you think this should be done, but perhaps a note of some sort might prepare the sober reader for a jolt.

I will write to Fr. Charles [Dumont of Scourmont] about the *Collectanea* [*Cisterciensia*]. I already wrote a small article on the subject. I think it fulfils a very necessary function, with the *chronique*, etc., but the articles are often below par. Perhaps the best thing would be to get more articles from good writers outside the Order while others are learning how to do it. But I would think it a pity if it were suppressed. *Monastic Studies* is in trouble in this country. As everything is veiled in secrecy or at least in ambiguity, I am not quite sure what is going on, but the future looks bleak. We cannot count on an American monastic magazine yet, in this Order. And the Benedictines still do not provide what is needed.

In October we are having a meeting of Abbots here. I have to speak on the mentality of modern youth and their capacity to fit in to the monastic life: or of the monastic life to accept them. It is a complex subject, probably different in different countries. Here I think that youths who are psychologically insecure and lost are placed in an ascetic machine that was designed for men of strong character and powerful egos. The result is not too wonderful. We suppress them when we ought to try to educate and develop them. Have you any ideas? Certainly the expedient of TV and recreation (of an artificial kind) will be worse than the sickness it is supposed to cure.

Hans Urs von Balthasar has sent me his *Herrlichkeit* [Lordship] and it is magnificent.* I am very glad to have it, though I read it very slowly and not with ease in German. It is great theology and everywhere perfect for monks—completely sapiential.

THOMAS MERTON TO JEAN LECLERCQ

September 28, 1964

There are many things to tell you but this must be a brief letter. The North American Abbots and novice masters are meeting here next week. A good idea but I think it will be rather a confused and frustrating experience. I wish you were here to contribute a little light and guidance. There seems to be a lot of confusion and some animosity over issues like whether the priest

---

*In an undated P.S. to a letter from Basle, Switzerland, Leclercq writes to Merton: "I spent last evening with H. U. von Balthasar, Munsterplatz 4, Basle. By the way, he mentioned you. He likes your writings. I suppose you know him, one of the best thinkers of today. I suggest that you send him some of your mimeographed essays (Rahner's Diaspora, etc.) and some poems (he likes them), and he will send you whatever of his you would like. (He translated in German parts of Claudel, Newman, and Peguy.)" Later von Balthasar translated into German and published a selection of Merton's poems entitled *Grace's House*, which included Merton's poem of the same title.

should forgo his private Mass and go to Communion at the conventual Mass, etc. I think our chief problem is the problem of the Brothers. Here at Gethsemani the Brothers seem to realize that they have a better monastic life than the choir and they are very anxious to preserve the relative simplicity, freedom, and informality of their life. Some who pass from the choir to the Brothers in the novitiate are impressed with a greater sense of authenticity and spiritual peace in the Brothers' life here. Yet in other monasteries of the Order there is a problem and some of them are simply abolishing the Brothers altogether.

I have at least a faint hope that we might actually attempt to face the hermit question here. This is very confidential. But I am glad to say that in a recent conversation Father Abbot showed himself very open and understanding on this subject. This, it seems to me, is very encouraging. I hope it may be possible to do something and to plan something not only for myself but for others. If this turns out to be so, I think that it will constitute one of the most significant and far-reaching developments in American monasticism. Please don't discuss this with anyone yet, not even the Gethsemani men in Rome. But I would greatly appreciate your prayers. Of course, if an occasion comes to speak confidentially to Dom Ignace on the subject, I would appreciate very much your help with him! My idea is to have a committee for a hermitage with you as one of the advisors; also, the Superior at Snowmass is interested.

Another, even more important development, and still more confidential, is that a Jesuit in Japan who is an expert on Zen is very anxious to have me come to Japan for a few months to see the Zen monks and perhaps participate in some of their disciplines.* This, I think, would be extremely important and fruitful, but I am not sure how Father Abbot and Dom Ignace will finally look at it. I have submitted the request to them, and I hope they will consider it objectively and without too much fear of the "novelty." Really, this could be the kind of step in renovation and original development that the Spirit of the Council so urgently calls for. Naturally, if the General and you were to speak of this, I would want you to speak freely and say whatever you think.

JEAN LECLERCQ TO THOMAS MERTON

Clervaux
October 10, 1964

I pray for your meeting of Abbots and novice masters. I guess there will be some confusion, but it is already a good thing to begin to "talk" and to consult monks, at least in the person of the novice masters.

I am not surprised that the hermit question is pro-

*Fr. Heinrich Dumoulin, S.J., of Sophia University invited Merton to come to Japan to study Zen. He had written *A History of Zen Buddhism*, which Merton had read avidly. Dom James refused permission after having consulted the Abbot General.

gressing. We notice that everywhere. I pray for your meeting. Here also ideas are moving forward. We must be patient. All evolution requires time. But we must begin somewhere.

I am so glad about what you can do concerning the Zen monks. I do not know whether I shall have any opportunity to speak about this. I shall be in Rome, 21 Via di Torre Rossa, Rome 6, in about ten days' time.

I think Balthasar approaches most closely a really monastic theology.

I have just given the retreat at Toumliline and am now here for a week of talks and then shall be going back to Rome for my little bit of teaching in Sant'Anselmo. I have just been appointed as a member of the Commission of the Consilium Liturgium for patristic lessons in the breviary. I hope they will be in the vernacular.

THOMAS MERTON TO JEAN LECLERCQ

October 22, 1964

Many thanks for your most recent letter, and your news. It is all right if "The Monk in the Diaspora" goes into *Collectanea* [*Cisterciensia*], except that I think that most of those in the Order who are interested have read it, though perhaps not in French, and perhaps also the French-speaking Abbots will only be disconcerted. However, whatever you think best. I was thinking of writing up the notes of my talk to the Abbots' meeting into an article and perhaps that would go well in the *Collectanea*, though it will also disconcert many. I enclose the notes. They are a bit naive and oversimplified as they stand, but I could put in nuances, and will make quite a few additions.

The Abbots' meeting was lively and I think everyone was satisfied or at least glad that the meeting took place. It was also profitable to have the novice masters involved, and I think it is really most important for the novice masters in our Order to get around and get experience of other houses. Unfortunately, it seems that my Father Abbot refuses to let me travel and even insisted that the only way a novice masters' meeting could be held with me in it was for it to be held *here*. It is even likely that he opposed another meeting, since it would involve me traveling to another monastery. In general the other Abbots think this is quite amusing. I must admit that it seems to me quite odd, and I can't say I am flattered to have my Abbot give the impression that he does not trust me. However, if I don't travel to other monasteries of the Order I can manage to survive the blow, I think. That is not the deepest desire of my heart. I have seen one, and that is quite sufficient for my own personal needs.

There was a quite general openness and sympathy among the Abbots toward a "solution" to the question of solitude within our Order. At least a relative solution in which the concept of temporary solitude would be admitted as proper to us. There is, I think, a quite reasonable concern lest the genuine cenobitic idea be injured, and I personally am as convinced as anyone of the importance of the cenobitic life, since without it normally there can be no basis for further solitude. The hermit will be the exception, the cenobite will be normal, and it is important, I think, to present the extension into solitude as a normal and legitimate prolongation of what begins in the cenobium, and temporary solitude as a dimension of the *cenobitic* life itself. Thus the rare case of the complete hermit will later on come to be accepted with less difficulty. My own temporary solitude gets to be more and more extended, for which I am glad.

Your *Otia* [Leclercq's new book, "Leisure"] came yesterday and I began it immediately. It is just what I am looking for. A splendid book.

THOMAS MERTON TO JEAN LECLERCQ

The essay Merton refers to in the following letter is "The Case for a Renewal of Eremitism in the Monastic State," which was later published in Contemplation in a World of Action *(Doubleday, 1971).*

April 2, 1965

Forgive me for keeping your offprint on the letter of St. Peter Damian so long. I am returning it, together with a couple of new essays. In one of them, a not too competent survey of the hermit life, I have used this as well as other articles of yours, to which I refer in the notes. If you have any suggestions and observations I would be grateful for them. It was written before I had seen the excellent "votum" of Dom Winandy on the canonical status of hermits. This was prepared for the meeting of the specialists that is being held at New Melleray. I am not allowed to attend this, of course, and though at one time there was some talk of having it here, that was not allowed either. I have given up commenting on this sort of thing, or even thinking about it very much. I did ask for permission to respond to the invitation of Godfrey Diekmann to come to Collegeville with all of you in August. This, of course, was refused. I hope the meeting will be successful and fruitful. Would you be able or likely to stop off here during your time in America? I would be very happy to see you. But there is nothing special going on, except that I have hopes of living permanently in solitude if the General Chapter poses no great obstacles. At the moment I am sleeping in the hermitage and often spending the greater part of the day there, but I am still novice master. Hence I have to spend much time in the novitiate too.

The piece on the Council and monasticism is necessarily superficial. It was written for a volume of studies to be printed by a college in Louisville.

Fr. Charles Dumont has me doing *chroniques* on non-Christian monachism, etc., and I wonder if I could borrow an offprint of a piece you did on monachism in Islam in order to summarize it? There is another study on pilgrim monachism in Islam which is published in Morocco and which I hope to obtain from Toumliline, unless you have a copy you can lend me. I would be most obliged if you could let me have at least your article, for the *chronique*. Though I never got permission to go to Japan, I am getting a lot of books on Zen from different sources and this will provide interesting material.

This will bring you my warm good wishes for Easter and my prayers. Pray for me too, and give my best wishes to any of my brethren you meet around Rome.

JEAN LECLERCQ TO THOMAS MERTON

Rome

April 9, 1965

Thanks for your letter and for the news, which is not of the best, except from the point of view of holiness. We shall regret not having you at Collegeville. I suggested having the meeting at Gethsemani. It is a great mystery in the Church that the way for a man to be himself should depend upon a General Chapter. What would St. Benedict and St. Bernard have thought of that? It is surely a case like the one you write about in your essay on Fr. Perrin.* God knows, and nothing matters.

Of course, it would be a great joy for me to see you

---

*Fr. Henri Perrin, S.J., was a French worker-priest during World War II who volunteered to go to Germany. He finally left the Jesuits and was considering laicization from the priesthood when he was killed in a mysterious automobile accident. Merton had written a review essay on Perrin's autobiography, *Priest and Worker*, that he titled "The Tragedy of Fr. Perrin," which appeared in *Continuum* in 1965.

at Gethsemani. I shall be spending September and October in the United States, and it would be possible to stop off at Louisville if you invite me.

I am encouraging Fr. Francis Derivaux [a monk of Gethsemani studying in Rome] to continue working along the lines which are greatly dependent on yours. It is a cause in which we might appreciate your influence. I think this young generation will have to carry on the creative task of re-thinking monastic spirituality. They will be less amateurish than we were and will make better connections between historical knowledge and new trends in philosophy.

I have mailed you the volume on pilgrim monasticism in Islam together with a couple more books on Islam. In Briquebec, I met a monk who is deeply committed to Christ, interested in Islam, and knows a lot (he learned Arabic). But the interests of his monastery are supposed to be in Japan. Yes, do keep the offprint from Toumliline. It is just an outline for a long study for which I am collecting material. Keep the offprint from the Richter volume too where I stood up for you against Italian criticism. I shall be reprinting it in a volume of essays.

I am leaving on April 24 for a tour of forty-five days in which I shall be giving retreats and talks in African monasteries. Pray for me!

May 11, 1965

This is to thank you for the books and offprints, which arrived safely.

Above all I want to thank you for your generous defense in the German article. It is gradually dawning on me that there must have been more discussion and criticism of me than I have imagined. Perhaps it is just as well that I did not know about all of it, but I can imagine. In any case, reading your remarks was a salutary experience, in the first place because your frankness and goodness in taking up what must be in some quarters a quite unpopular cause gives me a sense of the charity and concern of the Church even for the least of her children. But in any case you are noted for defending unpopular causes [eremitical desires]. Actually, of course, there must be many ways of looking at this "case." In many respects my life and work are certainly very equivocal, and if anyone wants to measure me by "normal" standards it will be easy to find that I fail to meet requirements—like everybody else, because in the long run, what are normal standards, and who meets them, except superficially? Then, too, I am certainly a *Geheimnis* [mystery] even to myself. And I have ceased to expect anything else. Nor do I have any secret hope left of making complete sense out of my existence, which must remain paradoxical. Thus in the end I must do what everyone else does and fall back on the mercy of God and try, as far as I can, not to fail Him in His loving will for me. Certainly, if I tried to please everyone, I would fail Him, and if I am to please Him I must inevitably displease a lot of very earnest and well-meaning people. And I intend to continue doing this without scruple.

The inner contradictions of the Dom Calati people are in any case rather amusing.* *They* are the hermits and monks who have precipitated themselves with open arms toward the world. They blame me because I have refused to do this and have instead tried to get back into the desert. Yet the *real* source of their objection and anger is that after all the world is listening to me rather than to them. Which is really very funny indeed. And I don't think that I am entirely in contradiction with myself, because I have consistently held that a monk can speak *from the desert* since there is no other place from which he has a better claim to be heard. Oh well, it is all ninety percent nonsense anyway, but I am grateful for your Christian charity and for your encouragement, because there are certainly times when I can use it.

You know of course that Dom James is now at the General Chapter. In inviting you to come in September (or whenever you can) to give a couple of talks to the novices and juniors, I am not in a position to do so

---

*Dom Benedetto Calati, O.S.B. Cam., was teaching at Sant'Anselmo in Rome at this time and had criticized the writings of Merton, especially those on the solitary life. Leclercq, it turned out, rose to Merton's defense. See *The School of Charity*. Calati later had a change of heart, due no doubt to Leclercq's intervention on Merton's behalf.

fully officially yet, but I am sure that (though he will not be very happy about it) Dom James will not refuse me the permission and will support me in the invitation. I will make it fully official when he returns, so I hope you can plan to come.

It will be really quite useful for you to come in many ways, for us. There is a project now of a more elaborate kind of hermit establishment (on which the Abbot himself is suddenly quite keen, as he foresees the possibility of six-year terms for Abbots), in a valley about five miles away from here. A kind of laura [a colony of hermitages] might be set up there, possibly. This is all very nice, and taking the idea in itself I would have no objections. However, there are the following considerations:

1. The Abbot's plan for this is disconcerting. He wants the hermits to live there in *trailers*. Do you get the picture? This means bright modern little machines for living with all possible comforts, etc., etc. Not only do I find myself incapable of accepting it, but my friends think it is very funny.

2. I have considerable reservations about being in a group with other people, even though only four or five. It has distinct disadvantages and means less solitude than I would have and do have where I now am in the hermitage (which is ideal for my own purposes).

3. I am very much afraid that this "colony" will

turn out to be over-organized and that in the end we will end up there with Dom James running it like a little abbey and everyone under his thumb not able to move or breathe without doing so in the way that he would like. I know he is my Abbot, but I am very much afraid that I have never honestly been able to deal with him as with a "spiritual father" and it would be impossible for me to do so sincerely.

4. My suggestion to him is that he should make his foundation in Norway and concentrate on that for the time being. That he should let me give up the novices and live all the time in the hermitage, where I now am for part of the time in any case. That he put a temporary hermitage in the valley where he wants his "colony" to be and let different monks go out there for a few days at a time to see how they like it. Later, when all have more experience, we can think of something more definite. And I hope it will *not* be elaborate.

I thought I would let you in on all this while I had a chance to do so.

Problems in the various houses in our Order in this country continue and I have the feeling that some of the biggest ones have yet to be faced.

Monastery of the Ascension, Togo
Octave of the Ascension
May 29, 1965

I received your letter of May 11 on arriving from
Obout, the Trappist monastery in the Cameroons. Here
I am with the Benedictine monks and nuns; I do not
find words sufficient to tell you how immensely I am
enjoying my stay in this country with its freshness and
simplicity, its rhythm, music, color, sacred dancing,
charm, and poetry. I am constantly thanking the Lord.
Of course, this is not just aesthetic sentiment. What I
enjoy are the people, African monks and nuns, almost
all still young, postulants, novices, and some professed.
At Obout, there are twelve Africans—including the
sub-prior, the novice master, and his assistant—for six
Europeans. The monastic vocations have pure motiva-
tions: "To follow Jesus," "To serve God better," "To
live in charity." I am delighted with them, so uncompli-
cated, and grace is at work in them. I try to speak their
language, with no abstract words, more images than
ideas: biblical, patristic, and liturgical language. I shall
write my impressions. You may already have received
the article in *Irenikon*, which Mount Saviour has already asked to translate in *Monastic Studies* because it
is "refreshing," so they say. In fact, monastic usages,
observances are adapted, even in the Trappist monasteries. Everywhere there is the vernacular, which the
General Chapter has now allowed for your Order in

African and other foundations. The Superior at Obout had just got back from the General Chapter and gave me some good news: permission for hermitages within the enclosure. The orientation is good. But the administrative machinery is heavy and slow-moving. The near future will show whether your Order is able to create a new monasticism in Africa and renovate the old one elsewhere.

In Obout I read your *Révolution noire* [*The Black Revolution*] with a certain pleasure, though I found some of your allusions to "colonialism" oversimplified. You realize that I do not favor colonialism—not even missionary colonialism. But the state of things is not as simple as that.

Thanks for the offprints and essays you sent to Clervaux. I will read them when I get home.

[P.S.] I am enjoying immensely my stay at St. Maur's Priory, Hangar, P.O. Songea, Tanzania, which is the only entirely African monastery. The Prior, Fr. Gregory Mwageni, was my student in Rome two years ago. You are well known here, as everywhere. I would be glad if you would send them some of your books. Trappist life is flourishing in Africa, as everywhere: factories, tea plantations, dairies, including a few real men of prayer.

July 5, 1965

Many thanks for the offprint on African monasticism and for your letter from Togo. I am convinced, by both of them, that the purity of the life there must be something very inspiring. Of course, God will bless them more than other countries insofar as they are much poorer, much more dependent on Him, much closer to the nature He has made. I do not mean to imply by this that technology has something bad about it, but nevertheless I think that in the big and prosperous nations the problems of monasticism will be otherwise complex. To begin with I am becoming more and more convinced that true simplicity, in the depths of the heart, is almost impossible for an American or a European. Certainly they may be subjectively sincere and mean well, but the fact that they come from a society that divides man from the very start and fills him with conflicts and doubts must mean something. I am impressed by the fact that what aggiornamento has meant here has been doubt. And that is perhaps healthy, or healthier than the old rigid refusal to admit even the possibility of anything being questioned. Now that everything is questioned, and should be questioned, too many are realizing that there is nothing in the monastic life that they consider worth holding on to. And if that is the case, all right. We do not have to try to persuade them that they are subjectively wrong. But I still think we are perhaps here too ready to think that after all we can prove them all wrong by a few adjustments. Anyway, there is a profound distrust, and if it finally leads to monks becoming Christians and having faith at last, then God will be glorified by it.

I am delighted that your African essay will be in *Monastic Studies*. It reads like Cassian.

About your coming here: Fr. Abbot said that in September much of the time the diocesan priests will be on retreat and that is not a good time for visits. But the last week in September is all right, and so I extend to you the official invitation to come and speak to the novices at the end of September or early in October at your convenience. I note that you want a copy of *Jubilee* of October '64 and I will write to Ed Rice to send you one.

Yes, I was a bit surprised that the General Chapter even officially and publically admitted that a Cistercian could become a hermit without the Order collapsing. It seems definite that I will be able to do this, and I am in fact spending most of my time in the hermitage: but it is uncertain as yet when Fr. Abbot will let me give up the job of master of novices.

JEAN LECLERCQ TO THOMAS MERTON

Clervaux

July 10, 1965

Thanks, Father, for your letter of July 5 and for your invitation to address the novices. They are the audience

I like, and I shall surely gain by my contact with them. It would be possible for me to be in Kentucky during the last week in September or, better still, a little later on, in October. Would it be convenient for me to come anytime in the first half of October? However, I will let you know in due time.

I will send you the new paper I wrote after my second African trip. Yes, I am of the same mind as you, and I come to the conclusion that there must be two different ways of living the evolution of monasticism: one for the Old World, where monasticism is old, respectable, and complicated for complicated people; another for Africa, and perhaps elsewhere, for young, fresh, simple, and creative folks. And, of course, I am chiefly interested in the second group, to which belongs the future. But we must also love the Old World and help them to find as much simplicity of heart as they are capable of: we must teach them to live over and beyond problems. Problems are not to be suppressed but faced. We must never give way to doubt. This will be a test of real vigorous vocations.

THOMAS MERTON TO JEAN LECLERCQ

September 18, 1965

I have received permission to retire to the hermitage and have been there over a month now. It is working out very well. I go down once a day for Mass and dinner; the rest of the time I am here alone, and later I hope to be alone all the time. For the time being it is difficult to get Fr. Abbot to allow me to say Mass here.

For the first time in twenty-five years I feel that I am leading a really "monastic" life. All that I had hoped to find in solitude is really here, and more. At the same time I can see that one cannot trifle with solitude as one can with the common life. It requires great energy and attention, but of course without constant grace it would be useless to expect these. Hence I would very much appreciate your prayers. But in any case it is good to have this silence and peace, and to be able to get down to the *unum necessarium* [the one thing necessary].

It is a great pity I was not able to be at Collegeville. Some people think there is a conflict between solitude and rare, exceptional meetings of this kind. I do not. I think they go together, and I am not of the opinion that the hermit is supposed to be so superior to all others that he cannot profit by humbly listening to what they have to say and learning from them. In fact I am afraid that there is an element of unconscious pharisaism in our exceptional zeal for separation from the world here. But the principle does remain, and if God wills solitude for me I take it entirely on His terms. If He wants it to be absolute, that is fine. I am glad at any rate that you thought of saying a word on my behalf. I feel very ashamed for not having been able to come, especially because of this implication of "superiority," which is so silly.

Thanks especially for your offprints on the hermit life. I wish I had had them when I was writing my article, which from the bibliographical point of view is very incomplete.

I look forward to seeing you, though I suppose Fr. Abbot will make a lot of difficulties because I am a "hermit now and not supposed to see people," etc. He is delighted with this aspect of it.

I do hope to see you. If necessary, just come up to the hermitage; I think you know how to find it, or someone can tell you. But normally I will come down and see you in the guest house.

JEAN LECLERCQ TO THOMAS MERTON

St. Joseph's Abbey
Spencer, Massachusetts 01562
October 18, 1965

I am sending you a copy of these abstracts for Fr. John Eudes [Bamberger, a monk of Gethsemani]. Thank you again for all your kindness. Please give my best thanks to Dom James.

Everything went well in the Chicago meeting, as afterward in Belleville with three remarkable Brothers; then with Dom [Peter] Minard in North Carolina: a real monk. After that I went to New Boston, where, once more, I found new hopes: Cîteaux was like that at the beginning. Mount Saviour was like them twenty years ago. Now after success, approval, then suspicion and disapproval, etc. That's one of the advantages of knowing a bit of history.

Tomorrow I shall be lecturing at the Episcopalian Seminary, Cambridge, Mass. The Dean chose the topic: monasticism today! After that I shall be flying to Regina Laudis, to Mount Saviour, Toronto, Paris, Rome.

How I do thank the Lord for these two months of travel in American monasteries, so full of hope and problems.

THOMAS MERTON TO JEAN LECLERCQ

November 13, 1965

Happy feast: it is the day of all the saints of the Order, and I am sure you have countless friends among them since you have done so much to make them known. I know I have many too. I have an article on the Council and religious, a bit out of date unfortunately, coming out in *Humanitas* (Brescia). It is a translation of one that was in *New Blackfriars*, but I am toning it down, as I think I was too wild in the other. The Constitution on Religious sounded very good, but the absurd speech of Cardinal [John] Heenan on "lazy priests in monasteries" who do not come out and help the parish clergy was regrettable. He seems to me to be an odd character.

Thanks for the clippings. The one on the non-violent fasting women was, in part, a surprise. I did participate in a very mild way but as I did not know when they were fasting I was ahead of them, in September. Obviously I did not go ten days without food; I am not that ascetic. I took a week on ordinary Lenten fast as we have it here. I am sure they did much good. I got a letter from them, and it was very moving. I think this was one of the beautiful things that accompanied the Council.

Thus you see I got two clippings from Regina Laudis [Benedictine nuns in Connecticut]. They said they were sending a pamphlet but this I did not receive, at least not yet.

Thanks for your fine visit here. It has left many good effects and I was glad to see you. You went about doing much good in the American monasteries. I hope that monasticism in this country will fulfil its still very living possibilities.

THOMAS MERTON TO JEAN LECLERCQ

July 7, 1966

Thanks for your good card from Africa. I have sent some mimeographs and books to the monks of Hangar, and hope they will be able to get something out of them. I am always delighted to be of use if I can, and thus justify my miserable existence. Actually, it is not miserable at all and I am getting more and more roots in solitude, so that the hermitage is to me the only conceivable kind of life. I do not claim that I am an ideal hermit, but then neither was I an ideal cenobite. I will probably cause less scandal being hidden in the woods, hence everything points to the fact that I am where I belong. But it is really an excellent life. Time takes on a completely different quality and one really lives, even though nothing apparently happens at all. The direction is all vertical, and that is what matters, though at the same time one is not conscious of it.

Fr. Flavian [Burns] is having a hermitage built for himself and I think he will do well in it. This does not, however, mean that Dom James is entirely friendly to hermits, but at any rate he tolerates them.

After four months of unremitting and strenuously applied effort, I managed to get hold of a copy of the December *Worship* for April. It seems to have been both banned and burned around here. But I certainly appreciate your article and the fact that you included me in such a litany of monastic boat-rockers.

I very much like your article in the recent *Collectanea* [*Cisterciensia*] on the future role of contemplatives. In fact it is true that already in the U.S. the problem of leisure is crucial: there is no work for more and more of the youth. I am afraid the solution in the minds of some people is to put them in the army and send them to Vietnam. An active response. I am giving talks to the monks now on technology, Marxism, etc., etc. and their implications for us.

Clervaux

July 14, 1966

Thank you for your letter of July 7, which I found on coming back from Africa and Madagascar. It was a wonderful trip! The article in *Worship* came out also in the June number of *La Vie Spirituelle*. I think I received your previous letter where you mentioned the banning of *Worship*.

I plan to be free in the United States for about a week from August 28 until the Spiritual Institute meeting September 7–11. I shall be trying to give some talks in order to earn a little money to pay traveling expenses. Fr. [Bernard] Haring and I have accepted to earn our fares like poor men. But as I have to be back in Rome on September 12 for the meeting of African Superiors, there will not be much time for going around getting money. Providence will surely help as usual.

[P.S.] Have I ever mentioned to you the book by Fr. Aelred Squire, an English Dominican, formerly an Anglican, and now a hermit (a real one) not far from Clervaux? I think that perhaps *you* could help him, recommend him to a publisher, and perhaps write a Foreword. His letter [enclosed] explains the case clearly enough. I did in fact go through the manuscript and I found it full of scholarship and charm (they do not often go together).

July 21, 1966

Thanks for your two recent notes. I will certainly do what I can to help Fr. Aelred Squire to get his book attended to in New York. The best I can do is recommend that it be read sympathetically by various publishers. However, my first suggestion is this: you yourself have been published by Farrar, Straus and Giroux, 19 Union Square West. You will pass through New York in a few weeks. Why not call on Mr. Robert Giroux, one of the partners and a good friend of mine: say I suggested it, and talk to him personally? He would then take an interest and I think he would be disposed to take the book seriously. Though I do not normally accept to write Prefaces these days, I could probably manage an exception in this case (for a "saint of the Order," etc., etc.). If Farrar, Straus and Giroux does not accept the book, then I could try it on Doubleday, another big publisher. I think the Catholic publishers in this country would respond.

Since you are going to be here, I very much hope you can give us a day: I cannot ask officially as the Abbot is now absent, but I will mention it to him when he returns next week and if he says yes will write "officially." Do keep a day open for us if you can, until you hear from me. I will be glad to see you as usual.

I am having some books and papers sent to the nuns in Uganda, very gladly.

The summer has been pretty hot, but not bad. One

thing I miss is that I cannot do much manual work; I
have a bad arm and my back is still affected by the operation I had in March. I am glad to hear Fr. Aelred
Squire is a hermit; I did not know that. I hope he will
pray for me—and I will also remember him. I am afraid
I like the solitary life very much indeed and enjoy every
moment of it. My only fear is that the Abbot may decide that I am not living up to his expectations and
make me return to the community, though I don't think
he has any reason to really. But you never know. He has
become a little negative to hermits lately. Perhaps he is
getting too many requests.

JEAN LECLERCQ TO THOMAS MERTON

Mananjary (Madagascar)

August 16, 1966

I know now that I shall land down at Louisville Airport
on Saturday, August 27. It is late, but there is no earlier
connection from New York. That same morning I shall
have given the final two talks of the retreat of the
monastery in Parma. If it is possible to pick me up at
the airport at that time and drive me to Gethsemani it
would be all right.

If it is too late to meet me at the airport, perhaps
you could send a message for me to the AA desk in the
airport and tell me when I can be picked up and driven
over.

I hope to stay two or three full days at Gethsemani,

and I also hope that my visit will not interfere with that of Fr. Haring. I have now received his U.S. address: Dept. of Religion, Brown University, Providence, Rhode Island.

I shall finish here with a visit to Sept Fons, where I shall give two talks to the community for the Feast of St. Bernard, and then I shall go to the Monastery of Torrechiara (Parma).

I am more and more interested in attempting to integrate the new trends in Christology, biblical studies, psychology, metaphysics with reflection and interpretation of monastic spirituality. It is not easy, but nevertheless gratifying. I had a glorious time with Father [Henri] de Lubac a few days ago when we talked about all that. (Did you know that he encouraged your confrère working on Teilhard and St. Bernard?) I have also made some recent discoveries about St. Bernard. No new texts, but new insights. I shall greatly profit by a discussion with you about all this.

THOMAS MERTON TO JEAN LECLERCQ

Leclercq had sent Merton a volume titled The Future of Western Spirituality, *in which he defends Merton from the previous attack by Dom Benedetto Calati, who also taught at Sant'Anselmo College in Rome. Calati accused Merton of being outside the mainstream of Western monasticism with his emphasis on contemplative life and prayer, as well as his stress on the importance of re-establishing the eremitical life within the monastic Orders of the West.*

November 18, 1966

Yesterday your *Chances de la spiritualité occidentale* [The future of Western spirituality] arrived and I want to thank you very much for it. Though I have seen most of the articles, in fact all of them, in one form or other, it will be a pleasure to go through them all together. But of course I must above all thank you for pages 28–31, clearer to me in French than they were in the German version. Thanks for having the courage to defend someone that most people apparently don't know what to make of. That is an element of my solitude, but I do not grudge you bringing me this kind of welcome company. The desert is never absolute, or should not be! Seriously, it is a consolation to find oneself after all part of the Catholic Church and not excommunicated without appeal as Dom Benedetto Calati and others would apparently want me to be. Many thanks for your charity and, I think, your objectivity too. It helps me to evaluate my own life and my own position in the Church. I am also very grateful to Père [Hans Urs] von Balthasar for his generous Introduction, or rather Postface, to the little selection of my poems. The selection was good, the translations seem to me to be very well done, and I am happy with the whole book. With you and him behind me I can feel a little more confidence— not that I have yet made myself notable for a lack of it. Perhaps I have always had too much.

Reflecting on my critics once again: of course, they have no trouble at all finding faults in me, since I have frankly discussed my own faults in public. An *ad personam* argument is not too difficult under such circumstances. I would, however, like to see them meet me on my own ground. Let them write spiritual journals as frank as mine and see if they will meet the test of publication. I do not fear this kind of competition, because I know it will never exist, or not in the camp of these amiable integrists. However, I have continued to produce such, and another volume is on its way to you—with its faults and perhaps its merits. I trust the charity of my friends to find the merits. The book, *Conjectures of a Guilty Bystander*, is off to you today. I have an alternative title for it: The Subjunctives of a Guilty Bartender. It is not, however, a "spiritual journal" anymore. There is not much that can be called "spiritual" in it. This will of course cause more comment. Those who were irritated because I published a spiritual journal (like Dom Sortais, who is no longer there to complain) will now be more irritated because this one is not spiritual. The children in the marketplace.

Jacques Maritain was here in October and we had a fine visit. He is very much a hermit now, and his latest book has added a hermit voice to the contemporary harmony (or disharmony). *Le Paysan de la Garonne* [*The Peasant of the Garonne*] is, I think, very fine. I think you would like it. I have heard from your friend Dom Gregory in Tanzania and will write him soon. Also, we had a true Sufi master from Algeria here. A most remarkable person. It was like meeting a Desert Father or someone out of the Bible. He invited me to come and talk to his disciples in Algeria but I told him this would be quite impossible. Yet I would love to talk to them in fact, and also to see some monasteries in Africa. But I suppose that will never be allowed. No matter. The woods are all I need.

JEAN LECLERCQ TO THOMAS MERTON

Clervaux

December 12, 1966

Thanks for the last essays you sent. Work on! The A.I.M. [Aide à l'Implantation Monastique] is preparing a journey for me for next April–July. I shall be going to India, Vietnam (South!), Cambodia, Formosa, and perhaps farther still (Hong Kong?), to those monasteries whose Abbots (Tilburg, etc.) have asked me to be sent. I want to spend most of the time in Vietnam giving priority to the Brothers and Sisters of the monasteries in that country: six are of the Cistercians of the Common Observance. When in India perhaps I shall meet some of your friends.

Did I tell you about the little Benedictine monastery in Sweden (Karr, Sturefors, Sweden) where a group of my confrères and friends are beginning a simple life? If you could send them some books and papers they would appreciate it. They are poor.

You may have received my little *St. Bernard*. After

my article in *Gregorianum*, there has been a campaign in favor of "contemplative priesthood for monks." An article written against me has inspired a paragraph of a speech of our good Holy Father Paul VI. Several people, who do not doubt the Pope's right to speak out, wonder whether the motives invoked are valid. This is not a question of authority but depends on history and theological reflection. On the whole, this may stimulate new interest in the problem and provoke new research, the results of which can be foreseen. Pray that I remain obedient and free.

[P.S.] Give my hearty greetings to Dom James. I hope all is developing well in Chile. I have been asked to write on the hermit life in the Review of the Sacred Congregation of Religious! *Haec mutatio dexterae excelsi!* [Change of the right hand of the most high!]

THOMAS MERTON TO JEAN LECLERCQ

February 17, 1967

Forgive my long delay in answering your pre-Christmas letter. I was swamped by letters in December and am barely recovering. But I want to get this off to you before I go to the hospital next week for a minor operation. Nothing of any importance.

Your proposed Asian journey sounds fascinating. I hope you will see Dom Bede Griffiths—and please give him my warm regards. I am doing some writing for

Gandhi Marg in New Delhi these days, but you will probably not run into them.

I thought I had sent some books to your monastery in Sweden. I am sure I did, but I will send more things to make sure. On the other hand, it is one thing to send books from here and quite another to have them arrive. One never knows what happens to mail.

Your "little *St. Bernard*" is perhaps one of the most attractive and lively of introductions. Above all, I am glad to hear that you will say something in the Review of the S. Congregation on eremitism. I was glad to see the little *Lettre de Liguge*, but I did not think any of the hermits really said anything important. Still, it was a touching and simple thing and a consolation to find others felt pretty much the same.

With Rome as it is, renewal will always be a slow struggle. The whole conception of authority all down the line is not favorable to a really spontaneous renewal, but we can be glad that things are as good as they are and not worse. The dead concepts will continue for a while to usurp the place belonging to life, but I do not think it will really matter much—except that some monasteries may finally be closed down. Perhaps that will be for the better.

I will see that the Swedish monastery gets some books and papers. Keep me in your good prayers: let us all hope we can manage to be at the same time obedient and free. It is not easy. But God is faithful, and that is my only hope.

Clervaux

[Undated—Spring 1967]

Thank you for sending books to Sweden. You know that surface mail is slow, especially at the Christmas season. But they will surely let you know when they receive them. They are faced with a new problem: unemployment is beginning in Sweden, and so immigration has been stopped. The non-Swedish members of the community have not had their visas renewed. But they are peaceful and confident, and the Lord will intervene. Two Taize Brothers are now living in a fraternity of the Virgin of the Poor in Kiluye, in Lake Kivu, Rwanda. In India, I shall be limiting myself to monasteries (Griffiths, Le Saux), but every name, address, recommendation you might send me could be useful. The article in the S. Congregation Review will not be at all striking: it must be very smooth, even sweet, with some play, the Roman way.

But we must begin to obsess people with the idea that eremitism has a right to exist legally and with freedom. As I told you, they will probably not accept my paper, because I am in favor of an independent eremitism, outside the dying eremitical congregations. But I'll tell them that I'll publish it elsewhere.

Several of us think that some (perhaps many) monasteries will be closed within the next ten or fifteen years, and there will be a new start from scratch. I had a long chat with the students of Monte Cistello. They are well oriented, and the future belongs to them.

I am going back to Rome on March 16 just for a talk at the Gregorian University on "The Future of Monasticism." Jesuits are more "clairvoyant" about our problems than are our own leaders. Perhaps this is because they are free from "our tradition."

JEAN LECLERCQ TO THOMAS MERTON

Vietnam

May 23, 1967

I am glad to leave this country of Vietnam after twenty-six days of anger. Not because of the war, which in the South is pretty enjoyable for many people, mainly the rich (including, of course, churchmen, religious, and monks). Everyone, except the poor, makes profit out of it. In religious houses I found excellent American food everywhere; ugly but enormous convents and monasteries are being built. The dollar has introduced a new religion in all circles. I had very few contacts with Buddhists, Confucianists, Animists, and members of non-Christian religions because "Christianity," as they say here, is a small and rich minority, closed in on itself, in contact only with politicians and businessmen. I have no idea at all what the *real* Vietnam thinks. I cannot help thinking that God knows what and why He is preparing for this country in the near future, whatever may be the military outcome of the war. In spite of all that there seems to be strong faith among the poor, a very simple faith which is either instinctive or personal. They will have killed people as did and still do the Buddhists, and probably among them there are a couple of real martyrs.

Yesterday, with a Father of the Missions Etrangères in Paris, I visited two villages of mountain people (Asiatic Indians, like the American Indians). Hardly any Vietnamese or Catholic priests take care of them, even though there are so many priests here. The only ones who care for them are the Protestants (Evangelists) and the French Missionaries. *Ubi est caritas?* [Where is charity?]

JEAN LECLERCQ TO THOMAS MERTON

Benedictine Monastery, Thien An
[Undated—May 1967?]

It is a joy for me to hear that your books, translated here, give a good idea of the U.S. in this country. That compensates and redresses the image given of your country by other Americans . . . All the novices in this monastery have received a copy of *Seeds of Contemplation*. They all greet you through me.

THOMAS MERTON TO JEAN LECLERCQ

June 7, 1967

I don't know if you are still in the Philippines or whether you are on your way back to Europe. I chase you with this letter because nowhere in your letter do I find the address of Thien An. On your envelope is another place, Thien Hoa. I do not know if they are the same but I suspect they are different. However, as this is a Benedictine community I am having some books sent there, but wait for confirmation of the address before writing Padre Marie José and sending some mimeographs.

Yes, it was good that in the Vietnamese translation of *No Man Is an Island*, they dared to print the Preface I had written!! I am happy. But that does not make the situation better there, and I am not sure whether it is a good thing to give a good impression of the U.S.A.— can one do so without a certain amount of ambiguity? There is always the chance of everything breaking out into world war there.

Nothing especially new here. The General Chapter is going on. I know there are some progressive Abbots in the Order, and there may be some hope, but here the feeling is rather one of quiet desperation: but that is because we are not really kept well informed and still have the impression of being "politically" manipulated. I would say that the spirit of the community is a little dampened after a few months' struggle for progress which have shown that there is much fair speech but not much chance for real action. However, I only get what I hear, and I do not get involved in it all. Where I am, there remains a fair chance of hesychia [a quiet form of prayer] and that is all that I ask, so that I may wait for the Lord at His coming, and be watchful. I will not write more, as I am not sure this letter will reach you—except perhaps after a long roundabout journey.

Vichy

June 29, 1967

Thank you for your private and circular letters [general mimeographed letter sent to many friends]. I flew back from Djakarta to Vichy via Singapore, Bangkok, Bombay, Karachi, Athens over the finishing war in the Near East, where I did not even know there was a war. It was only when we heard that we could not stop at Cairo that I found out! Now, after a short rest, I am flying to the Conference of Anglican Religious in Oxford. Then I shall be in Clervaux for six or seven weeks. From there I shall go to Mauritania, the United States, and Canada. Of course, I now have on Christian and non-Christian monasticism in Asia quite a dossier of texts, ideas, and images. I do not know whether I shall have time and the opportunity for writing anything. In the meanwhile I mail you my journal for the second month of the trip, which includes the longest part on Vietnam. This journal is made up of letters to my Abbot.

In my opinion Vietnam is not an occasion for world war (there are so many other occasions if they really want a war), but it is a very bad way of going about war on the part of the United States. Notice that I am not saying the war is bad: all wars are bad—even crusades.

I agree with you about the General Chapter. Tomorrow I am going to Sept Fons and I shall probably learn more about it. But I do not have much confidence. The head is too old, and the mechanism too perfect. Yet, surprisingly enough, though I had no hopes or illusions, I was astounded by the good work done by our Congress of Abbots: the next session might well turn out to be a good thing. We are leading now. You have more fervor, but we have more culture. And piety does not meet every need.

July 2, 1967

Many thanks for the booklet about the charming little Abbey of St. Vincent de Chantelle. I wrote to you in the Philippines to ask the right address of the monks in Vietnam to whom books are to be sent. I hope the letter was forwarded to you somewhere. You did not give me the address, I believe. Or did you? I was not sure of the address on the envelope which was crossed out.

I have heard from Dom Placide Deseille and want to write to him. His new foundation [Eastern Rite Foundation] sounds to me like one of the few really hopeful things that has happened among Cistercians. The General Chapter seems to have had no serious orientation whatever. But I cannot judge from partial reports.

Hope you are well. Will we see you later on this year?

I have finished a short commentary on Camus's book *The Plague* for a Protestant publisher. And am reviewing [Henri] de Lubac's book on Teilhard, which I think dots the i's and crosses the t's. I wonder increas-

ingly if our Fr. Gerard [Bryan] can get very far with re-
lating Teilhard and St. Bernard: yes and no. But the
School of Chartres might be more hopeful, don't you
think? However, I have no intention of starting on such
a project myself.

THOMAS MERTON TO JEAN LECLERCQ

July 18, 1967
I have just finished reading your collection of letters on
your Asian journey. Quite an experience! This is a
memorable document and it could form the nucleus of
a most interesting book. I hope that something more
will come of it. How about working it up into a book
using the material in the letters as a basis for a more
amplified treatment—before the details slip out of your
memory? And with more development of your monastic ideas. I am sure Bob Giroux, at Farrar, Straus and
Giroux, would be very interested.

You give a very clear and forceful impression of the
Church's situation and problems there. And I was glad
that the picture of monasticism was, in the main, hopeful. I will be happy to help in any way by sending
books to anyone who can use them. Keep me informed,
and I will send things. The picture you give of Vietnam
was very depressing in a way (though the monks
looked good). I am glad you are coming to this country
at the end of the summer and hope to see you.

It was comforting to note that all the places where

you found some reality and life of prayer were places that had at least some remote connection with Cîteaux (as, for example, the foundations of La Pierre-qui-Vire), and I am glad the Trappists of Indonesia were good. Of Kurisumala I had long had a very good impression, but I was happy to learn of the others. As to the corruption that American civilization is bringing with it—that is a source of more and more sorrow to me. One feels this corruption even here, in spite of all the good there still is in the country and in this monastery. Yet there is a stink of decay, not the decay of oldness, the enfeeblement of something past its prime: but rather a splendid cancerous fulness that shines with a kind of health, a richness, and a flowering of something overgrown, overdeveloped, and lacking in basic intelligence, above all in living wisdom. Here in the monastery we have a sense of struggling with futility even in the midst of great opportunity. There is now being introduced an elaborate game of dialogue in which the monastery will be divided into groups like communist cells in which everyone will discuss how to discuss, and when they have finished that will discuss possible changes: thus changes will be put off indefinitely, in the name of "discussion." It will take time to organize the cells and to make sure that they are properly indoctrinated, that they have the suitable frame of mind, etc.

My own life goes well. I have finally obtained permission to say Mass at the hermitage, though I will also sometimes say Mass at the monastery and occasionally concelebrate.

I hope you will come down here. Let me know and I will send the "official" invitation. I'd like you, if possible, to meet a woman theologian [Rosemary Ruether] who has some strong ideas about monasticism having "lost its soul" (she is a radical eschatologist and works with Negroes) and it would be great if we could have a little discussion on this. She hopes to be here around the end of August.

JEAN LECLERCQ TO THOMAS MERTON

Clervaux

July 20, 1967

I have just come back from a Conference on Monastic Liturgy at Orval: one hundred monks and cloistered nuns, O.S.B. and O.C.S.O. The whole of the offices and Mass (including the Canon, with permission) was in the vernacular. What beauty! There was a wonderful hymn by Patrice de La Tour du Pin, with a perfect melody. I had to take refuge in the tribune, so as not to dance in choir. Up in the tribune I could do it clandestinely, seen only by God. The Abbot of Timadeuc was there. I spoke on the dialectic law-prophetism in the Old Testament, in Christ, in the Church: of the necessity there is for both a "liturgical commission" making laws and research people looking to the future.

Before that, I had been to the Conference of Anglican Religious at Oxford, where I gave a talk. We were in the big pseudo-Gothic hall of Christ Church: I was dressed as much as possible in secular clothes and introduced by an entirely violet-clad Anglican Bishop. I tried to shake up these comfortable medieval people, who seemed unconscious of the fact that the streets beyond the walls were no longer the same as I had known them five years ago.

I am going to a new foundation, Rorchinard, in Vercors, France, which I have been following for twenty years and from which Erbach came. Now the Abbot of St. Wandrille thinks it is time to give them a free status and has asked me to go and see them. Orval is preparing a foundation. On my way back I'll show them my slides on Asiatic monasticism (Buddhist, including Zen, Christian, and Cistercian) to give them ideas.

I asked the Abbot of Timadeuc about Placide Deseille. His impression was good. I trust the man.

Another excellent thing started by a Trappist out of the Order, but with the help of his Abbot so far, is the ashram of Francis Mahieu of Scourmont in collaboration with Bede Griffiths.

JEAN LECLERCQ TO THOMAS MERTON

Clervaux

August 8, 1967

First, thank you for your kind judgment of my letters from Asia. I plan, during my flights in the U.S. next month, to write my impressions on Asian monasticism. We shall see what the result is.

The last news of the Kurisumala ashram is that they are preparing for a foundation in about one or two years' time. The episcopal conference has asked them to prepare a new Indian Rite. That is important!

As for America in Asia, we must not forget that for them U.S. equals West equals Christianity.

JEAN LECLERCQ TO THOMAS MERTON

Clervaux

August 29, 1967

Thank you for your letter of August 19. I maintain the date I fixed the weekend of September 9–10, unless I hear to the contrary from you while I am in Mount Saviour between September 4 and 9. But I can stay until the 11th if you want me to do so. On arriving I shall meet Mother Adele Fiske, who was in India at the same time as I, but she stayed longer and went to the northern countries, where there are more Hindu monks. We want to pool our information. I am sure I shall learn a lot from her.

Thanks for the article on solitude. Even the Sacred Congregation of Religious published two articles this year in their review *Vita Religiosa* about the hermit life. One of the articles was by me: I did not think that they would accept it because they now want to control everything, and I wrote in favor of hermits not organized into congregations. In the meantime I met by chance the new secretary of the Congregation, Msgr.

[Antonio] Mauro, who was very nice. Having less personal ideas than Msgr. [Paul] Philippe, he may be a better secretary and stay within his bounds.

The number of *Rythmes du Monde* 1964, 4, finally came out. It deals with the meeting of African Superiors in Rome last year. There is an excellent paper by Abbot André Louf on the future of monastic canon law.

Glad that the Vietnam material looks all right. I fear that I am right.

JEAN LECLERCQ TO THOMAS MERTON

In August 1967 Pope Paul VI requested that Merton write a "Message of Contemplatives" that would be presented to the Synod of Bishops in the fall of the same year. It stressed the importance of the contemplative dimension of the Church in the world today. As it turned out, the "Message" became a joint work of Merton collaborating with another Cistercian monk, Dom André Louf, and Dom J. B. Porion, the Procurator General of the Carthusians.

Carmel du Reposoir
October 28, 1967

I have just commented on the "Message of Contemplatives" to the Synod, in this wonderful Carmel with such a beautiful name (an old charterhouse), when Fr. Reginald Gregoire showed me your letter. I shall probably have an opportunity for commenting on the new items of "*L'actualité contemplative*" in some review. I would like to mention discreetly your contribution to this message. What parallels with your books could you suggest? Or (and) what other ideas have you? Help me.

[P.S.] By chance I came across and read in *Collectanea* [*Cisterciensia*] 67, 3, your reviews on Zen. Did you know that A.I.M. is preparing a congress of monastic Superiors in Bangkok, where I hope we shall invite Hindu and Buddhist monks and nuns? I have written a report, inspired by my letters, which I shall submit to you. In New York, I shall meet Mother Adele Fiske, who has just come back from Asia, and John Moffitt.

THOMAS MERTON TO JEAN LECLERCQ

November 10, 1967

Sorry to have been silent so long. I have been over my ears in letters, etc. and cannot handle it. I was sorry when Dom James said you had written him that you were ill and needed an operation. I hope you are better. It was a pity you could not get to this country. But I hope we will see you next time.

Thanks for your interest in the "Message of Contemplatives": I thought it had fallen completely flat. I have heard absolutely nothing about it. I am sending a copy of the draft I wrote when requested to do so. Then another thing I wrote after it. Also a couple of other pieces. I don't know what books of mine would correspond to what was said there except that those ideas crop up everywhere in what I write. Especially, however, *New Seeds of Contemplation* (which corrects the errors of perspective in the earlier version) says a lot of what I have been trying to say. Also *The New Man.* The material is also in *The Ascent to Truth*, but that was from my point of view an "unnatural" book. I was trying to be academic or a theologian or something, and that is not what I am.

At the moment I am writing more and more poetry and studies that deal with primitive religions.

I am very interested to hear of the big meeting in Asia. In a way I wish I could be there. Yet I am coming to a kind of inner decision on this question, in case I may need it later. Dom James is retiring here—to the immense relief of everyone!—and it is likely that the next man will be much more liberal in regard to going out to conferences and so forth. I get innumerable invitations which I have to refuse, and my decision is that since I am a hermit I shall continue to do so. That is to say that I will not appear anywhere in public or semi-public, anyhow. Do you agree that this is a good decision for me? I think it is best that I stay out of the mainstream of things and mind my own business. It is true, I will fail to learn things and be less informed, but I think it is my lot to engage in something else and do my own work, quite apart from what others may be doing. In other words, Dom James has succeeded in his policy of insulation and I will not get involved in monastic affairs. It seems that his greatest fear for me has always been that I might go around monasteries talking and spreading "dangerous" ideas. I think that now, however, my "dangerous" ideas are not needed and are even a bit old-fashioned.

Keep well, peace and joy! I keep you in my prayers. Pray for me. And for all of us here as we approach our turning point.

JEAN LECLERCQ TO THOMAS MERTON

Vanves (Seine), France
December 30, 1967

Thanks for the papers you sent me. I gave the envelope to a confrère who had heard in Rome that you had left the priesthood and who had asked me what you had become. He could see where you were.

I came to St. André in Brugge to prepare the A.I.M. meeting in Bangkok '68. We prepared the program, chose the periti [observers] to invite or to contact. I suggested that we invite you, and everybody was delighted. You or (and) your Abbot would receive a letter on that purpose. The meeting has been postponed until next December for various reasons. And it must be carefully prepared. I think that if you would go to just one place, this would be the one: the meeting will be entirely monastic (O.C.S.O., O.Cist.) and focused on the encounter of Christianity with Hinduism and Buddhism. I obtained that instead of being just a party of organization, about practical problems, or of intellectual encounters, it would be first of all a spiritual experience at a certain level of exchange between the various religions. I think that it might work out. Of course, your very presence would be a sign and a help.

Can you imagine that I have been appointed to a commission of ten members to prepare a papal document on "the contemplative life and the enclosure of the nuns"? Is it not already revealing that the two realities are associated? Much to do. More a question of tactic than of thought. No nun in on the commission. Pray for us and for them.

Now the Brothers of Belleville [experimental house in Illinois] have been visited by the General, who was well impressed. But they must firmly maintain the lay character of their community. Does the priestly ministry prepare one to be a Superior?

I met Dom André Louf and others who told me the history of the "Message of Contemplatives."

I am interested by your article on Brother Pascal [in *Jubilee*], whom I had met in Grandselve [abbey in France] just before he left, and we had talked. Then he wrote to me, and I recommended him to a Bishop just before he died. Sad case of what may lead the lay Brother system.

All your papers on renewal and openness are excellent. Balthasar wants to publish a volume of my monastic articles in German. Pray for me.

Greetings to your new Abbot, whoever he is.

January 14, 1968

Annuntio tibi gaudium magnum: habemus abbatem [I announce with great joy: we have an Abbot]—I waited for the election before replying to your letter. Fr. Flavian [Burns] is our new Abbot. Certainly the best man we have for the job at the moment. He is certainly also the one who will most understand the A.I.M. meeting, and I think that eventually he will consent to my going. I am most anxious to attend the meeting and believe it will be very fruitful. Certainly I am convinced that it is very important for me to meet some Eastern monks and also see some of our own Christian monasteries out there. I pray that this may be realized, though I fear that Thailand may be involved in war by December! Not sure, though. There is always hope that some glimmer of sanity will still prevail in Washington.

Unfortunately, if a letter of invitation has already reached Dom James, who remained in charge until the last minute and is still here as "advisor," then he will have sent a negative reply. I have heard nothing of course. I suggest you write personally to Fr. Flavian about it perhaps.

The election was only yesterday and has not yet been confirmed, but I suppose it will be by the time I get this letter mailed.

As soon as I get a chance to talk over matters with Dom Flavian, I shall make the following proposal: that I should be allowed to make one discreet and fruitful monastic journey each year, lasting about a month or six weeks, visiting monasteries of other religions and traditions and also some of our own. This one to the A.I.M. conference would be the one for 1968. What do you think? Such journeys would always be kept quiet and there would be no "public" talks or anything like that. I feel this would be something quite necessary at the present stage of my vocation, don't you? I mean not only for myself but for others, as this sharing is essential. If you agree, perhaps you might mention it to him.

I certainly keep your commission for the papal document in my prayers. Have you seen the recent correspondence in the *N.C.R.* [*National Catholic Reporter*]? I can send copies if you haven't. Surely someone will have sent it all, the article by Colman McCarthy and the various replies from Cistercians. I think I'll send a copy of the replies anyway, as I have one.

JEAN LECLERCQ TO THOMAS MERTON

January 21, 1968

Thanks for the good news. And for the contemplative forum, I heard of it but had not read it. I understand now why, a few days ago, a reporter from *Time* interviewed me during two hours for an article to be published this week on "the crisis of the contemplative Orders." He consulted three people in Rome, including a Trappist. At the end I asked him if what I had said coincided with what the other two had said. He replied, yes, except that the Trappist did not mention that some had left the Order. Of course, he knew quite well: N.C.R. had given the figures. O truth!

I agree with the *monachus (=abbas) indignans* [N.C.R. respondent] that the responsibility is in Rome, but not (only) in the Vatican. This also has been the concern, and still is, of all the Abbots. But no more of that for the moment.

I enclose an invitation for you to Bangkok, addressed to Dom Flavian. Explain it to him. Abbot [Marie] de Floris, President of the A.I.M., will come to Rome at the end of January to contact the Propaganda, the Secretariat for non-Christian religions, Abbot Primate. I will send you a formal invitation with program, etc. when I receive them. One of the problems is that our financial means are limited, and we cannot afford many people. I suppose you could consider coming at your own expense, or get a grant, or some fees for a couple of talks given in Tokyo or elsewhere?

My plan is to go to Bangkok via the States and Japan to contact some Zen monks. Wouldn't it be marvelous to be over there with you?

By the way, do you know of any possibility for me getting some sort of grant for this journey of contacts with Asian monasticism?

On my way back I would stop in Ceylon, where there are a few Benedictine nuns and plenty of Buddhist monks. The nuns were founded by the courageous and intelligent Madre Dore, who criticized you. Did I tell you that I saw her recently in Sardinia? I told her that her article was *"un chef-d'oeuvre de méchanceté féminine"* [a masterpiece of feminine naughtiness]. We spoke of you. She is a good lady. In twenty-five years she has made foundations in Nigeria, Argentina, Ceylon, and in two places in Sardinia.

Of course for you this journey would be an occasion for opening and stimulating minds in Japan, Indonesia, and elsewhere. I think Japanese Trappists are in particular need of "disoccidentalization."

A young Ceylonese priest brought me yesterday his thesis on "Separation from the World in Buddhism Compared with Christianity." Nice work by a fine boy.

In April or May 1969 will take place the third (every three years) meeting of African monks, probably this time in East Africa (Kenya or elsewhere). Would this not be your second round?

Give my best regards to Dom James. He has always been kind, understanding, and generous toward me, although I have not always been easy to handle. When I become a hermit, I will go under his guidance.

[P.S.] Looking at the general situation of monasticism and inter-religion relations today, I think you've been cut off long enough and the Church needs you to go out and share with others, not only in writing. Your very personality (and some say the same of me, but of course I am not a giant) is a witness of the liberty in Christ, and that has to be *shown*.

January 30, 1968

Many thanks for your letter of January 21 about the Bangkok meeting. I have discussed it with the new Abbot, Dom Flavian. As yet the discussion has been inconclusive. Dom Flavian is quite open to the proposal, but does not believe that he has the authority to simply grant me permission for this journey. No problem of money, but he is a bit timid about possible reactions at Monte Cistello. However, he has definitely said that if someone could bring cogent reasons to bear, he will gladly consent. In other words, perhaps the Secretariat could make clear to the Abbot General that this is important as well as perfectly "monastic." Are Cistercians of the S.O. participating? That too would simplify matters, if others are engaged in it.

Here are people who would probably be helpful: the Archbishop of Louisville. Perhaps Abbot de Floris (or you for that matter) could write to the Archbishop suggesting that he persuade our Abbot of the importance of this? Or the Abbot General, someone in Rome. I think perhaps even Cardinal [Egidio] Vagnozzi, though very conservative, would support this, as he is interested in Asian religions and seemed to approve my own work in that line when he was here.

As to getting funds: I'm sure the Ford Foundation would willingly finance some of your projects, but I do not know their address and do not know much about how to get money out of them, as I have never tried. I suggest that the next time you are here we might discuss the matter with some friends in Louisville, in academic circles, who know all about this. Or I could refer you to one of them if you like. Let me know.

I really wonder if by next December Thailand will be enveloped in war too. Of course that need not make too much difference as regards the conference, unless it happens to be a large-scale war with China, etc.

I do hope that I can participate in it with you, and would love to travel out there with you via Japan. Also of course I would very much like to be at the African meeting. It is necessary that I finally learn something about what is going on, and attendance at these meetings is one essential way of getting some reliable information.

Thanks so much for your efforts to help me. I hope Dom Flavian will see his way to backing it all the way.

JEAN LECLERCQ TO THOMAS MERTON

Clervaux

February 2, 1968

Thanks for your letter, which I received today. I read it to Abbot de Floris, who brought me the program I am able to send you today. I think he will write to Dom Flavian. Today we met people of the Propaganda and tomorrow we shall meet those of the Secretariat for non-Christian religions.

Of course, members of the [Cistercians] S.O. will be

at Bangkok. The Superior of Rawa Seneng [Trappist monastery in Indonesia] was one of the most interested in the project. We hope there will be Trappists from Japan, Hong Kong, etc. A Trappist contribution is absolutely essential.

I understand the hesitations of Dom Flavian. But he is your Abbot. And who is "Monte Cistello" (and who will it be next fall)? Here is an example connected with the Patristic Conference at Oxford: an Abbot asked the General if he could send someone. And the answer was no. Another Abbot told me, "I never ask. I have always sent someone, and I shall send [someone again]."

Things are going badly in Vietnam. I pray. Pray too for the poor monks over there. Repression after American corruption will be horrible. I am sorry for them. I tried to keep them free from the dollar. Now something is going to be done, but too late, I am afraid.

THOMAS MERTON TO JEAN LECLERCQ

March 9, 1968

I am afraid I cannot yet give any definite answer on the Bangkok project. Fr. Flavian has not said no, but he has not said yes. He is quite timid and non-committal about it. I do not think in the first place he has any realization of the importance of this meeting and he regards the whole affair purely as a matter of making a "concession" to some supposed instinct for activism. He says he is willing to make this "concession" provided that he has enough pressure put on him from persons in positions of importance or authority. If Abbot de Floris wrote to him, and if someone else of importance (including yourself) wrote direct to him urging strongly that I be present, he would probably consent. It is also important that someone in the Order write to him. I have written to Dom Willibrord at Rawa Seneng to put a little heat on.

This puts the problem as simply as I can formulate it at the moment.

The "monastic study" group project is of the greatest interest. Let me keep the notes on it for a while and reflect on them. I will write to Fr. [Raimondo] Panikkar. If such a group is ever formed, I would be very interested in participating.

I have a very great problem about staying in America (U.S.A.) and thus to some extent remaining identified with a society which I believe to be under the judgment of God and in some sense under a curse for the crimes of the Vietnam War. On the other hand, I do not see how leaving the country can be fully honest either. I have asked to be sent to our foundation in Chile, and this was refused. But it would not be a real solution. I might also go to the very small monastic foundation of a former novice [Ernesto Cardenal] of Nicaragua. I could be a hermit there. But this too might be equivocal. I hope to speak to you about all this sometime. Perhaps if this society is under judgment I too should remain and sustain myself the judgment of everyone else, since I am after all not that much different from the others. The question of sin is a great one today—I mean collective guilt for crimes against humanity.

What you say of Thien An breaks my heart. I think of those poor monks, to whom I felt close, and to whom I had written not so many months ago. I shall certainly pray for them very earnestly, especially in the Eucharist. They too were destroyed by my country, in the eagerness to "save them from communism"!!!

If I get any definite decision from Fr. Flavian, I will write to you about it.

Thanks for everything.

JEAN LECLERCQ TO THOMAS MERTON

Clervaux

June 1, 1968

Nothing new, except that the former Prior of the Benedictine monks of Thien An has been killed in Saigon by our (American) bomb.

[P.S.] I have just come back from a tour of the English monasteries. In Caldey [Welsh monastery] and elsewhere, one voice: "Bring Tom to us!" There is no one who has not been influenced by you, Tom.

Could you send me on loan McLuhan's *Interpreting Mass Media*?

June 14, 1968

Thanks first of all for *Ecclesia saltans* [drawing for a journal], who will appear in due course dancing on *Monks Pond*. The magazine has been very well received in poetic circles—where there is quite a sense of community! I will confine myself to four numbers however. Much very good material has come in. Is it perhaps the first avant-garde poetry magazine put out by monks in our time? At any rate, it seems to flourish in the monastic climate.

Now to business. Fr. Flavian has still decided nothing about my going to Bangkok, because he says he received no official invitation. A letter from you was, however, lost in Chile, and that might have contained something. He says that he cannot let me go if I am not officially invited. I said your invitation was enough.

However, Bangkok or no, I have been permitted to go to preach a retreat at Rawa Seneng before the time of the meeting, so I will be in the area, and I very much hope to take the opportunity to visit non-Christian monastic centers in the Far East insofar as it may be possible. There are many opportunities and I am writing to a friend who has many Buddhist, etc. connections. This time I would like to confine myself to SE Asia and Japan (not India).

The other thing is that in May I was able to go out to Redwoods, where I found a very nice community and had a good week of conferences with them. I was also able to go on the Pacific shore, which you have probably seen, and which is very desolate. I am hoping to get permission from Fr. Flavian to spend Lent there (there is an empty house that is available). It is the best solitude I have seen so far.

Thanks for your note from Clervaux about England, etc. Maybe someday I will get to Europe, but at the moment I think I have to set careful limits, and go out only to monasteries in Asia, Africa, or South America, where there is a special need (and where, incidentally, I can learn more). They really have no need of me in Europe; plenty of experts all over the place. But I feel that in these other countries I should help as far as I can. So I don't want to get involved in anything in Europe and the U.S.—and I do think solitude retains top priority for me, especially if I can find a real desert place like the Pacific.

If Fr. Flavian gets an official invitation I suppose he will let me go to Bangkok, though for some reason he seems hesitant. As to Rawa Seneng he has no problem, as he says the General Chapter permits one to preach retreats in other monasteries of the Order. I do not fully understand all his hesitations but I respect them.

THOMAS MERTON TO JEAN LECLERCQ

Abbot Flavian Burns finally did receive the formal invitation and gave Merton the necessary permission to go to Bangkok. Leclercq responded briefly to Merton's question about what would be expected of them in Bangkok for the conference of Asian monastics, indicating that Merton would speak on "Marxism and Monastic Perspectives," ending in a lighthearted way: "We will clown together!"

July 23, 1968

Thanks for your good letter about the arrangements for Bangkok. I will be glad to give the talk on Marxism and so on. Important indeed!! I've familiarized myself pretty well with Herbert Marcuse, whose ideas are so influential in the "student revolts" of the time. I must admit that I find him closer to monasticism than many theologians. Those who question the structures of contemporary society at least look to monks for a certain distance and critical perspective, which, alas, is seldom found. The vocation of the monk in the modern world, especially Marxist, is not survival but prophecy. We are all too busy saving our skins.

On the morning of December 10, Merton spoke to the assembled Asian Superiors in English on the agreed subject of Marxism and monastic perspectives. His address was recorded by both Dutch and Italian TV and was later published as an Appendix in The Asian Journal of Thomas Merton *(New Directions, 1973). Most memorable for me was his parting advice: "If you forget everything else that has been said, I would suggest you remember for the future: 'From now on, everybody stands on his own feet.'"*

In the middle of the afternoon of December 10, Thomas Merton was found dead in his cottage room with a defective standing fan, still running, lying across his body. He was pronounced dead by a medical doctor "as a result of heart failure induced by electric shock." The remains were flown back to the Abbey of Gethsemani, where a funeral liturgy was celebrated on December 17. His grave is marked by a simple white cross like those of all the other monks buried there during the past century and a half.

APPENDIX

CHRONOLOGY:
JEAN LECLERCQ

✠

1911 Born January 31 in Avesnes, northern France.

1917 Spent several months with family at Lourdes.

1928 Toward end of August entered the Abbey of Clervaux in Luxembourg.

1931 Made temporary profession as a Benedictine monk of Clervaux.

1932 Called to military service in France.

1933 Sent to Rome to the new foundation of Clervaux at San Gerolamo. Made retreats at Frascati, the Camaldolese monastery outside Rome. Visits to Ostia and Hadrian's Villa.

1937 Studies at Sant'Anselmo ended. Began studies in Paris.

1938 Taught dogmatic theology at the Abbey of Clervaux.

1939 Was a noncombatant soldier in the French military service.

1940 Given monastic shelter at the abbeys of Hautecombe in Savoy, En Calcat, and Liguge. Published translation and introduction to Smaragdus of Saint Mihiel, *La Voie royale; Le Diadème des moines* (La Pierre-qui-Vire, 1940–1949).

1941 Began work, which lasted until 1945, at the Bibliothèque Nationale analyzing manuscripts and writing descriptive notes for each.

1942 Published *Jean de Paris et l'ecclésiologie du XIII siècle* (Vrin).

1946 Published *La Spiritualité de Pierre de Celle, 1115–1183* (Vrin), *Pierre le Vénérable* (Saint-Wandrille), and, in collaboration with Jean Paul Bonnes, *Un Maître de la vie spirituelle au XI siècle: Jean de Fécamp* (Vrin).

1948 Published *Analecta Monastica*, First Series, Studia Anselmiana, 31 (Pont. Institutum S. Anselmi), *Saint Bernard mystique* (Desclée de Brouwer), and *La Vie parfaite* (Brepols), which was published in the United States in 1961 as *The Life of Perfection* (Liturgical Press).

1949 Published *Lettres d'Yves de Chartres*, critical edition with introduction (Les Belles-Lettres).

1951 Published *Un Humaniste ermite: Le Bienheureux Paul Giustiniani (1476–1528)* (Camaldoli).

1953 Published *Analecta Monastica*, Second Series (Pont. Institutum S. Anselmi), *Etudes sur S. Bernard et le texte de ses écrits* (Apud Curiam Generalem Sacri Ordinis Cisterciensis), and *La dottrina del beato Paolo Giustiniani* (Frascati).

1955 Published *La Vie érémitique d'après la doctrine du bienheureux Paul Giustiniani* with a Preface by Thomas Merton (Plon), which was published in the United States in 1961 as *Alone with God* (Farrar, Straus).

1957 Published *L'Amour des lettres et le désir de Dieu* (Cerf), which was published in the United States in 1961 as *The Love of Learning and the Desire for God* (Fordham University Press). In collaboration with C. H. Talbot and H. Rochais published the first volume of the critical edition of St. Bernard of Clairvaux, *Sancti Bernardi opera* (Editiones Cistercienses).

1958 Published second volume of *Sancti Bernardi opera* (Editiones Cistercienses).

1959 Published *L'Idée de la royauté du Christ au moyen âge* (Cerf).

1960 Published *Saint Pierre Damien, ermite et homme d'Eglise* (Edizioni di Storia e Letteratura). Also published a typescript privately reproduced and distributed by the Benedictine Institute of Sacred Theology of St. John's University, *The History of Medieval Spirituality*.

1961 In collaboration with François Vandenbroucke and Louis Bouyer published *La Spiritualité du moyen âge* (Aubier), which was published in the United States in 1968 as *The*

Spirituality of the Middle Ages (Desclée and Seabury Press). Also published *Etudes sur le vocabulaire monastique du moyen âge* (Studia Anselmiana).

1962 Published *Recueil d'études sur Saint Bernard et ses écrits* (Edizioni di Storia e Letteratura).

1963 Published *La Liturgie et les paradoxes chrétiens* (Cerf), the third volume of *Sancti Bernardi opera* (Editiones Cistercienses), and *Otia monastica* (Studia Anselmiana).

1964 Published *Aux sources de la spiritualité occidentale: Etapes et constantes* (Cerf).

1965 Published *Témoins de la spiritualité occidentale* (Cerf).

1966 Published the fourth volume of *Sancti Bernardi opera* (Editiones Cistercienses), *Chances de la spiritualité occidentale* (Cerf), and *S. Bernard et l'esprit cistercian* (du Seuil), which was published in the United States in 1976 as *Bernard of Clairvaux and the Cistercian Spirit* (Cistercian Publications).

1968 Published *Aspects du monachisme hier et aujourd'hui* (Editions de la Source), which was published in the United States in 1978 as *Aspects of Monasticism* (Cistercian Publications). Also published the fifth volume of *Sancti Bernardi opera* (Editiones Cistercienses).

1969 Published *Vie religieuse et vie contemplative* (Duculot), which was published in the United States in 1978 as *Contemplative Life* (Cistercian Publications).

1970 Published *Le Défi de la vie contemplative* (Duculot). Also published the first part of the sixth volume of *Sancti Bernardi opera* (Editiones Cistercienses).

1971 Published *Moines et moniales ont-ils un avenir?* (Lumen Vitae).

1972 Published the second part of the sixth volume of *Sancti Bernardi opera* (Editiones Cistercienses).

1974 Published the seventh volume of *Sancti Bernardi opera* (Editiones Cistercienses).

1976 Published *Nouveau Visage de Bernard de Clairvaux: Approches psycho-historiques* (Cerf), which was published in the United States in 1990 as *A Second Look at Bernard of Clairvaux* (Cistercian Publications). Also published *Libérez les prisonniers: Du bon larron à Jean XXIII* (Cerf).

1977 Published eighth, and last, volume of *Sancti Bernardi opera* (Editiones Cistercienses). (Also available on CD-ROM: CETEDOC Library of Christian Latin Texts CLCLT-1 [Brepols, 1991].)

1979 Published *Monks and Love in Twelfth-Century France: Psychohistorical Essays* (Clarendon Press).

1982 Published *Monks on Marriage: A Twelfth-Century View* (Seabury Press).

1983 Published *La Femme et les femmes dans l'oeuvre de saint Bernard* (Téqui), which was published in the United States in 1989 as *Women and Saint Bernard of Clairvaux* (Cistercian Publications).

1985 In collaboration with Bernard McGinn and John Meyendorff published *Christian Spirituality: Origins to the Twelfth Century* (Crossroad).

1986 Published *Nouvelle Page d'histoire monastique: Histoire de l'A.I.M., 1960–1985* (Aide Inter-Monastères).

1989 Published *Bernard de Clairvaux* (Desclée) and *Umanesimo e cultura monastica* (Jaca Book).

1990 Published *Esperienza spirituale e teologia: Alla scuola dei monaci medievali* (Jaca Book).

1992 Published *Il monachesimo occidentali oggi* (Abbazia San Benedetto).

1993 Published *Regards monastiques sur le Christ au moyen âge: Jésus et Jésus-Christ* (Desclée), *Momenti e figure di storia monastica italiana* (Centro Storico Benedettino Italiano), and *Di grazia a grazia: Memorie* (Jaca Book), which was published in the United States in 2000 as *Memoirs: From Grace to Grace* (St. Bede's Publications). Also published *"Ossa humiliata" I: Frammenti di spiritualità monastica* (Abbazia San Benedetto).

Died on October 27 at Clervaux.

1994 *La figura della donna nel medioevo* (Jaca Book), a selection of articles, was published.

2000 *Lettere di Dom Jean Leclercq* (Badia de Santa Maria del Monte) was published.

CHRONOLOGY:
THOMAS MERTON

✠

1915 Born January 31 in Prades, southern France, to artist Ruth Jenkins of Zanesville, Ohio, and watercolor artist Owen Merton of Christchurch, New Zealand.

1916 Baptized in Prades with Dr. Tom Bennett of London as god-father. Moved to Maryland and New York. Lived with mother's family in Douglaston, Long Island, New York.

1921 Mother's death from cancer in Bellevue Hospital, New York.

1922 Attended elementary school in Bermuda.

1925 Traveled to France with father. Residence at St. Antonin.

1926 Entered Lycée Ingres, Montauban, France. Spent Christmas with father and the Privat family in Murat, France.

1928 Returned to England and entered Oakham School, Rutland, the next year.

1931 Father's death from brain tumor. Stayed with godfather, Tom Bennett, in London.

1932 Graduated from Oakham; received scholarship to Clare College, Cambridge University.

1933 Traveled to Italy; spent summer in United States; entered Cambridge in the fall to study modern languages in preparation to get into British diplomatic service.

1934 Gained second in modern-language tripos, part 1, at Cambridge. Moved back to New York after a dissipated year at Cambridge.

1935 Entered Columbia University in February. Befriended Mark Van Doren, Robert Lax, and Edward Rice, among others.

1939 Received M.A. from Columbia. Taught English composition in University Extension at Columbia and later at St. Bonaventure University until 1941.

1940 Met Baroness Catherine de Hueck (Doherty); went to work at Friendship House in Harlem, New York. Traveled to Cuba.

1941 Made Easter retreat at Gethsemani at the suggestion of Dan Walsh. Entered the Abbey of Gethsemani on December 10.

1944 Made simple profession of vows on March 29. Published *Thirty Poems* (New Directions), which was arranged by Mark Van Doren.

1946 Published a second volume of poems, *A Man in the Divided Sea* (New Directions).

1948 Published *The Seven Storey Mountain* (Harcourt, Brace), *Figures for an Apocalypse* (New Directions), and *Exile Ends in Glory* (Bruce).

1949 Ordained priest at Gethsemani on May 26. Published *Seeds of Contemplation* (New Directions), *The Waters of Siloe* (Harcourt, Brace), and *The Tears of the Blind Lions* (New Directions).

1950 Published *What Are These Wounds?* (Bruce).

1951 Appointed master of students in May. Became an American citizen on June 22. Published *The Ascent to Truth* (Harcourt, Brace).

1953 Published *The Sign of Jonas* (Harcourt, Brace) and *Bread in the Wilderness* (New Directions).

1954 Published *The Last of the Fathers* (Harcourt, Brace), on St. Bernard of Clairvaux.

1955 Published *No Man Is an Island* (Harcourt, Brace), and was appointed master of novices until 1965.

1956 Published *The Living Bread* (Farrar, Straus).

1957 Attended a meeting at St. John's Abbey, Collegeville, Minnesota, and met Dr. Gregory Zilboorg. Published *The Tower of Babel* (New Directions), *The Strange Islands* (New Directions), and *The Silent Life* (Farrar, Straus).

1958 Published *Thoughts in Solitude* (Farrar, Straus).

1959 Published *Selected Poems* (New Directions) and *The Secular Journal* (Farrar, Straus).

1960 Published *Spiritual Direction and Meditation* (Liturgical Press), *The Wisdom of the Desert* (New Directions), and *Disputed Questions* (Farrar, Straus).

1961 Published *The New Man* (Farrar, Straus and Giroux) and *The Behavior of Titans* (New Directions).

1962 Published *New Seeds of Contemplation* (New Directions) and *Original Child Bomb* (New Directions).

1963 Published *Life and Holiness* (Herder and Herder) and *Emblems of a Season of Fury* (New Directions).

1964 Met Dr. D. Suzuki in New York. Received honorary L.D. from the University of Kentucky. Published *Seeds of Destruction* (Farrar, Straus and Giroux).

1965 Given permission on August 20 to live in a hermitage at Gethsemani. Published *The Way of Chuang-Tzu* (New Directions) and *Seasons of Celebration* (Farrar, Straus and Giroux).

1966 Met Jacques Maritain at Gethsemani. Also visited by Joan Baez. Published *Raids on the Unspeakable* (New Directions).

1967 Published *Mystics and Zen Masters* (Farrar, Straus and Giroux).

1968 In May visited Christ in the Desert, New Mexico, and Redwoods Monastery, California. In early September and October returned to New Mexico and California and went to Alaska before heading to the Far East to attend the conference of religious Superiors in Asia, including three meetings with the Dalai Lama, and the Spiritual Summit Conference of World Religions in Calcutta, before addressing the participants of the Asian Benedictine and Cistercian Superiors at Bangkok, Thailand, on December 10. Several hours later he was accidentally electrocuted by a faulty electric fan. His funeral Mass was held on December 17 at the Abbey of Gethsemani. Published *Cables to the Ace* (New Directions), *Faith and Violence* (University of Notre Dame Press), and *Zen and the Birds of Appetite* (New Directions).

1969 *My Argument with the Gestapo* (Doubleday), *The Climate of Monastic Prayer* (Cistercian Publications), and *The Geography of Lograire* (New Directions).

1971 *Contemplation in a World of Action* (Doubleday).

1973 *The Asian Journal of Thomas Merton* (New Directions).

1976 *Ishi Means Man* (Unicorn Press).

1977 *The Monastic Journey* (Sheed, Andrews and McMeel) and *The Collected Poems of Thomas Merton* (New Directions).

1979 *Love and Living* (Farrar, Straus and Giroux).

1980 *The Nonviolent Alternative* (Farrar, Straus and Giroux).

1981 *The Literary Essays of Thomas Merton* (New Directions), *Day of a Stranger* (Peregrine Smith), and *Introductions East and West* (Unicorn Press).

1982 *Woods, Shore, Desert* (University of New Mexico Press).

1985 *The Hidden Ground of Love: Letters on Religious Experience and Social Concerns* (Farrar, Straus and Giroux).

1988 *A Vow of Conversation: Journals 1964–1965* (Farrar, Straus and Giroux).

1989 *Thomas Merton in Alaska* (New Directions) and *The Road to Joy: Letters to New and Old Friends* (Farrar, Straus and Giroux).

1990 *The School of Charity: Letters on Religious Renewal and Spiritual Direction* (Farrar, Straus and Giroux).

1993 *The Courage for Truth: Letters to Writers* (Farrar, Straus and Giroux).

1994 *Witness to Freedom: Letters in Times of Crisis* (Farrar, Straus and Giroux).

1995 First of seven volumes of journals was published, *Run to the Mountain: The Story of a Vocation*, Journals 1939–1941 (HarperSanFrancisco), as well as *Passion for Peace: The Social Essays* (Crossroad).

1996 *Entering the Silence: Becoming a Monk and Writer*, Journals 1941–1952; *A Search for Solitude: Pursuing the Monk's True Life*, Journals 1952–1960; and *Turning Toward the World: The Pivotal Years*, Journals 1960–1963 (HarperSanFrancisco).

1997 *Dancing in the Water of Life: Seeking Peace in the Hermitage*, Journals 1963–1965; and *Learning to Love: Exploring Solitude and Freedom*, Journals 1966–1967 (HarperSanFrancisco).

1998 *The Other Side of the Mountain: The End of the Journey*, Journals 1967–1968 (HarperSanFrancisco).

1999 *The Intimate Merton: His Life from His Journals* (HarperSanFrancisco).

2002 *Survival or Prophecy? The Letters of Thomas Merton and Jean Leclercq* (Farrar, Straus and Giroux).

INDEX